The Evergreen Community:

CREATIVE TEACHING IDEAS FROM *EVERGREEN* CLASSROOMS

to accompany

Evergreen: A Guide to Writing
Seventh Edition

Susan Fawcett

HOUGHTON MIFFLIN COMPANY   BOSTON   NEW YORK

Senior Sponsoring Editor: Mary Jo Southern
Development Editor: Kellie Cardone
Editorial Assistants: Peter Mooney, Celeste Ng
Production/Design Assistant: Bethany Schlegel
Senior Manufacturing Coordinator: Priscilla Bailey
Marketing Manager: Annamarie Rice

Printed in the U.S.A.

ISBN: 0-618-27388-3

2 3 4 5 6 7 8 9-VHO-07 06 05 04

Contents

1
Creating a Writer's Community

I predict that *Evergreen* will always be very high on the list of texts considered for our developmental composition course. The readings are an attractive supplement. Throughout, you present instruction, examples, and models written in an unbiased, nonsexist, and encouraging style. You really do have a winner in this textbook—hard to beat!

Linda Whisnant, Guilford Technical Community College, NC

From Margie Cronin, San Antonio College, TX

Establishing a Learner-Friendly Atmosphere

My students know from achievement test scores and from their own experience in English classes that they need to improve their writing, grammar, and communication skills. Many are frightened at being in an English class and have a valid dislike for anything at all that has to do with an English class.

From the first moment we meet, I try to establish a comfortable, relaxed, safe, positive, equitable atmosphere. I explain the goals and objectives in the course curriculum and describe how we will work to complete and achieve them. My students know exactly what is expected and how we are going to achieve that together. I continue to maintain this atmosphere throughout the semester; therefore, I have an excellent response from my students. When they realize they are in a nonthreatening environment, they feel free to be themselves, and they become creative and productive.

As a motivational technique, I read aloud essays written by former students, from the most recent classes I have taught. I pass each of the essays around after reading it, and we discuss it in specific detail in order to grasp why it is well written. I present an overview of the essay and dissect each stage of development in easy, simplistic terms. My classes thereby get to hear the sound of a good essay, see the format, and view in detail each example offered. I try to demystify the procedure and process for them; I even tell them this is show and tell. They laugh. I state that writing is a skill like any other and that we get better at it by practicing. I explain that I work to improve my writing and communication skills all the time. My students know I expect to receive essays of at least five paragraphs, and because I have this expectation, they rise to the occasion, expect more of themselves, and produce. Using this philosophy, attitude, and technique with my classes has always had positive results: outstanding essays.

Audience Awareness and Purpose

Use your imagination to write two different "pretend" postcards in the spaces below. The subject of each one should be the same: a trip you are taking. Write as if you are on the trip when you write. Although the subject matter for the two cards is the same, the audience and purpose for each one is different, explained for each card below.

For this first card, **write to a close friend,** someone who knows you very well. Pretend that your friend was planning to go with you on this trip, but that at the last minute had change his or her plans and had to cancel. **Your purpose is** to make this friend determined to never again miss a chance to go with you on a trip.

For the second card, **write to some authority figure** back home. This might be a parent, aunt, uncle, minister, coach, teacher, etc. Pretend that this person did not think it was really very wise for you to take this trip, for whatever reason. **Your purpose is** to convince this person that you are really getting something worthwhile out of taking this trip.

From Kathleen Beauchene, Community College of Rhode Island,

Learning the Syllabus

On the second day of class, I begin with a quiz—on
given them on the first day and asked them to read
about five questions; the first is always, "What is my
the answers, we review the syllabus. At the end, I
papers and submit them to me—my proof that I kn
course policies. Just an idea that works. (Plus, we all
they attempt to spell my last name!)

From Ray Foster, Scottsdale Community College, AZ

Look-Alikes/Sound-Alikes

Using Chapter 39, "Look-Alikes/Sound-Alikes," I assign all twenty-two groups of words to each student with the idea that each student will present one (or several) of the confusing pairs to the class for clarification. After some prompting, the students actually enjoy making the presentations. The classes seem to gain additional insights in how the words are used differently.

Those students who are reluctant to make an oral presentation (for whatever reasons) are asked to turn in the twenty-two groups of words with original sentences using the confused words for credit.

From Jane Wilson, Ivy Technical State College, IN

Class Project: Team Writing Exercise

We discuss Chapters 5 to 13 (developing the different kinds of paragraphs) early in the semester. At this point in the term, students are still not entirely comfortable with the class, their own writing skills, or their classmates. The intriguing picture at the end of Chapter 6, "Narration" (see p. 82) helps me alleviate some of these discomforts.

The class is divided into groups of five or six students. We first discuss how to write narration, and we spend some time asking questions about the picture and its characters. Each group is then asked to write a short story about the picture—one story per group, one grade per group.

Students who are shy about participating in a class brainstorming session find it much easier to respond in a small group. Ideas may come slowly at first, but they soon flow freely (and sometimes hilariously). Most students get caught up in the enthusiasm of the situation.

The next step in the group's writing process is deciding which ideas to use and which to discard—a useful skill for a writer. In this part of the process, the students are learning the art of compromise and are developing team-work skills.

At this point, one student is assigned to put the story on paper as the group dictates. Once the initial effort is on paper, the editing process begins. Many times peer or group editing efforts fall short of the goal because students have difficulty with constructive, honest criticism. (It is so easy to say to another student, "This sounds all right to me.") With a common grade hanging in the balance, however, the participants are more likely to point out errors or concerns. When there is disagreement, some of the groups actually consult the text for help.

The stories I receive are extremely entertaining and imaginative; however, the real benefits of the project go far beyond the stories themselves. By the time we have completed this exercise, the students have lost (or at least reduced) their fear of exposing their ideas and skills to the scrutiny of their classmates. They have learned to look up answers to their own questions, and they may have gained some knowledge about grammar and mechanics and the writing process.

I have found this assignment to be a definite "win-win" situation!

From Suzanne Doonan, Pennsylvania Institute of Technology, PA

The Biography Poem

The biography poem has been a successful activity that I've used to enhance students' self-esteem and to provide a publishing opportunity. It works best with a small, cohesive, trusting group. I introduce the activity by modeling the writing process. Depicting the class group as having a distinctive personality, I solicit descriptions of class traits and a name for the group. I demonstrate writing, revising, and editing the poem on the chalkboard. Then students write their own biography poems for a class publication.

Chatterboxes

Funny, sarcastic, truthful, sincere
Students of Mrs. Doonan
Lovers of learning and people
Who feel blessed and determined
Who fear rejection and failing
Who would like to come out on top
Friends

The Group Chapter

The group chapter—a chapter that I work through with the entire class—allows the instructor to designate a time for whole-class discussion or collaborative work on specific topics. Suggested topics:

Unit	*Evergreen* Chapters	Topics
I	1, 2	Prewriting
	3	Rudiments of the paragraph
II	4	Paragraph unity
	14, 16	Mini-essay
III	14	Parts of the essay

The suggested chapters can be assigned so that students will be prepared for class discussion to be held at least once a week.

Peer Editing

The use of peer editing derives from an understanding of revision as the process of "seeing again." When students share their ideas, they begin to see that their writing does have worth. Second, they become more aware of audience and purpose. Finally, if approached in a positive manner, students readily offer constructive criticism to their peers, as well as support. Several methods of peer editing have been tried:

1. As a group, students are asked to draw up a list of positive comments to make about their peers' writing. They use the list to comment on one another's work and are then encouraged to put their comments in writing.

2. The instructor distributes a list of questions for students to answer about a writing assignment. Here are some examples: What is this paper about? What has the author stated well? Do you want more information about a particular incident? Can you suggest other examples, support, or evidence that the author might include? Students exchange papers and answer the questions in writing. Papers are returned to the original owners for revision.

3. Student papers are collected, names are removed, and the papers are redistributed randomly. Peer editors then map the papers. Both the original paper and the map are returned to the author. The author has the opportunity to add information on the basis of any gaps in the map.

Additional information about peer editing is available in *Beat Not the Poor Desk* by Marie Ponsot and Rosemary Deen (Boynton/Cook Publishers, 1982).

From William G. Thomas, Los Angeles Trade Technical College, CA

Creating Community in the Classroom

I begin the term referring both to the beginning and the middle of the text. This weaves together the "concepts" of paragraph building and the rhetorical approaches to writing, grammar, spelling, punctuation, and other mechanics. The author selections are used for critical reading, and students respond to questions suggested as well as to others that may be relevant. Many of my students, since we are primarily an inner-city, vocationally oriented college, are foreign-born or have had a "Swiss cheese" education in English. Accordingly, reading with comprehension is new, and important, to most of them.

The drills are completed as part of the weekly homework, along with one or more written assignments each week. I use "learning groups" or "teams," much like a writers' workshop, so students assist one another and interact a great deal. Our weekly routine, for our three one-hour sessions, includes: day one—first draft, which the team members review with one another while I serve as a consultant; day two—second draft, where students discuss their respective improvement techniques; and day three—-the selection by each group of their "best" paper, which, if time and other class commitments allow, is read by a representative student from the group. The class as a whole votes on the best paper, but students are not allowed to ballot for their own teams' papers. I reward winners with candy bars, pens—whatever inexpensive items I can find as bribery.

For the drills, which we use on a daily basis, drawn directly from *Evergreen,* the teams, usually six in number, compete in turn and receive plus or minus points for their answers. Every few weeks, I add up the scores and once more play the bribery game.

Intermittently, and at the end of the semester, I check each student's *Evergreen* to ensure that *all* assignments have been completed. I insist that if they expect me to be prepared to teach, they must be prepared to learn.

At the last class meeting, prior to the final examination, the students evaluate the class with no holds barred. Our objective is to collectively suggest improvements from which future classes will benefit. *Evergreen* consistently draws raves and for all the right reasons.

From the above, you can readily imagine why I plan to continue the use of this fine developmental English text, as well as to use its garden-titled (*Grassroots*) companion in other developmental classes.

From William G. Thomas, Los Angeles Trade Technical College, CA

Cross-Cultural Community

As a term paper in my developmental English class (which uses *Evergreen*), I require the preparation of a cross-cultural paper by each student. The topic can be any aspect, characteristic, feature, or person (or whatever) of a culture other than one's own. We also eliminate the U.S.A. because we're already in that culture. Thus, a twenty-year-old from El Salvador, majoring in nursing, might write about childbirth practices in India. A Los Angeles native could choose education in Costa Rica; a Mexican American, chastity in Ethiopia—the subjects have been endless.

The process is uncomplicated. After almost three-quarters of the semester has passed, students feel quite comfortable with the classroom environment, with one another, and with me (if they still laugh at all my jokes). For up to six class sessions, students from a particular area of the globe—Asia, Central America, the Caribbean, South America, Africa, and Europe—serve as a panel (much like *Meet the Press*). They tell their classmates a bit about their native countries and why they came to the United States, and provide examples of common and different cultural practices and major historical events.

Recently, we had a Caribbean panel with one fortyish student who had spent four years in a Cuban prison, and the Asian panel included an older student who, as a South Vietnamese army lieutenant, was captured by the enemy and spent seven years in a prison camp. The world of the past confronted all of us in the realities and personal experiences that were shared.

From Karen O'Donnell, Finger Lakes Community College, NY

Cooperative Learning Activity

First, I have to introduce to my students the concept of group roles, those of recorder, observer, encourager, researcher, and checker. The recorder takes notes and is the record keeper. The observer watches how well the group works together and notices whether all group members are participating. The encourager helps draw other students out by saying such things as "What do you think?" or "Tell us more" or "What is your idea?" The researcher looks up information for the group when necessary and gets and returns supplies. The checker makes sure everyone understands, keeps everyone on task, and seeks help if necessary. I give all students a handout explaining all the roles, give role cards to each group during cooperative activities, and randomly assign roles and switch roles for other activities.

To actually teach prewriting, I use cooperative groups. First, I divide the class into groups of three, four, or five members, using some random basis; this depends on class size. The ideal is four to a group. This will form base groups. Next, I have the groups count off (1, 2, 3, 4; 1, 2, and so on), then I have the ones group together, the twos group together, and so on, to form the expert groups. Each expert group will be assigned to learn one of the first four types of prewriting activities in Chapter 2 of the text *Evergreen* by Susan Fawcett: freewriting, brainstorming, clustering, and asking questions. Each expert group will develop the topic *college* (or any other chosen topic), using their individual method of prewriting so that they can bring an example back to their base groups. I randomly assign roles to each member of the expert group.

When the expert groups are finished, each member, returning to his or her base group, teaches the prewriting activity just learned. (I also randomly assign roles in the base groups.) Then the base groups develop another topic, such as *writing,* using all four of the prewriting skills, and the results are hung on the walls of the classroom. I find this technique very effective because there can be transfer from short-term to long-term memory through the use of rehearsal and recoding.

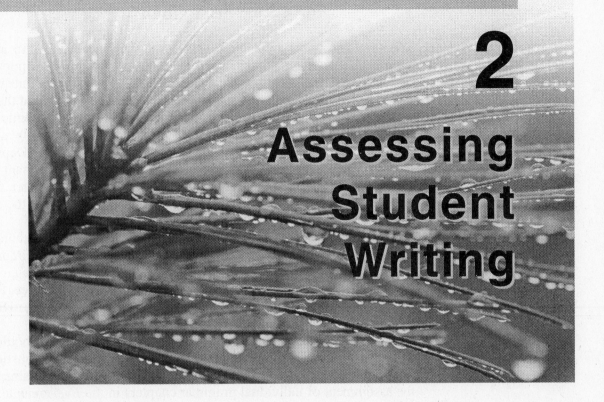

2
Assessing Student Writing

The greatest strength of *Evergreen* is its comprehensive coverage of writing skills, its excellent reading selections and examples, and its use of "stand alone" chapters that permit instructors to organize instruction as best suits their needs.

Meredith A. Wilson, Solano Community College, CA

The effective content in each section of *Evergreen* has allowed me to use one text instead of three for instruction on the writing process, grammar and sentence structure, and summary writing based on readings.

Margaret Koenig, Monterey Peninsula College, CA

From Patricia Malinowski, Finger Lakes Community College, NY

Diagnosis

The first step in teaching the college composition course is to assess the writing abilities of each student. At a community college, our population is drawn from a multitude of educational backgrounds. The students who have enrolled in this course have been advised to do so on the basis of their scores on the reading placement test (Descriptive Test of Language Skills [DTLS], published by the College Board), a writing sample (evaluated by a member of the Humanities Department and the Developmental Studies Department), or prior academic record. Because of this diversity, it is important to establish the skill level of each student at the beginning of the semester. Once this assessment has been made, the instructor can best facilitate the student's individual growth.

On the first day of class, after briefly explaining the college composition course to the students and distributing course outlines and requirements, the instructor can have students take one, two, or all three of the diagnostic tests below and on page 15. Judging from instructors' past experience, two diagnostic paragraphs are an adequate sample. Follow up with the Diagnostic Survey on page 16.

Once the student has completed this process, the instructor should be able to assess the student's capabilities, both in the framework of holistic writing and in regard to specific grammar problems. From this assessment comes the assignment of individual grammar chapters in the *Evergreen* text.

Sample Diagnostic Paragraphs

Diagnostic Paragraph I

Write an essay about one of the following topics. Hand in all your work. Simply underline any words that you do not know how to spell.

1. Give your impressions of a recent concert you attended: the crowd, the performers, or the music.

2. Is television harmful or not? Use specific examples.

3. Describe a law you believe is unfair and explain your view.

4. What changes would you make at your job, at your school, or in your family?

5. What movie, book, television program, or concert has made a strong impression on you, and why?

Alternative Diagnostic Paragraph I

Write a paragraph about one of the following topics. Hand in all your work. Simply underline any words that you do not know how to spell.

1. People do various things to relax. Describe what you do to relax and explain why you think it is the best method of relaxation.

2. We have all met, at some time, an unusual person. Describe such a person and explain why that person is unique.

3. Describe a place you like to visit and offer reasons why someone else would enjoy visiting that place.

Diagnostic Writing II

Over the past several years, different government commissions and independent research organizations have found that the American educational system is declining. Different groups have cited various reasons for this decline.

Read the article on the back of this page.* Use your own experiences to either agree or disagree with the author's thesis regarding education and the direction of education in America.

Use the space below for outlining or organizing your ideas.

Diagnostic Paragraph III

Interview one of your classmates.

Using the information you have obtained in your interview, write a paragraph in which you introduce your classmate to the entire class.

---

* Stanley Thompson, "Students Responsible for Failure to Learn," *Los Angeles Times.*

Diagnostic Survey

Answer each of the following questions.

1. How do you feel about writing?

2. Why do you feel this way?

3. What are your strengths and weaknesses in writing?

4. What have you done to strengthen and improve your writing skills?

5. List any college writing or English courses you have taken.

6. Additional comments:

From Patricia Malinowski, Finger Lakes Community College, NY

College Composition Writing Outcomes

Writing is a process, and below are means of measuring students' outcomes.

Unit I: The student

- Indicates mastery of the paragraph:

    Develops one idea well.

    Uses a topic sentence.

    Has appropriate supporting details.

    Can "close" ideas.

- Can use simple sentences; indicates ability to use compound sentences.

- Can begin to use rhetorical patterns of description and narration.

- Makes grammatical errors, but they do not interfere with the expression of ideas.

- Makes spelling errors; indicates ability to identify them.

Unit II: The student

- Indicates mastery of the mini-essay:

    Keeps all points under mastery of the paragraph.

    Can also write adequate introductory, body, and concluding paragraphs.

- Can use simple and compound sentences; indicates use of complex sentences.

- Can use several rhetorical patterns.

- Is starting to identify grammar problems independently and correct them.

- Indicates ability to correct spelling errors.

Unit III: The student

- Indicates mastery of the multiple-paragraph essay:

    Can develop a thesis.

    Can give the thesis adequate support.

- Can use transitional words and phrases, a variety of sentence patterns, and several rhetorical modes.

- Makes fewer grammatical errors; has ability to correct errors and work through multiple revisions.

- Shows an increased confidence in writing abilities.

Conference Component

One important component in this course is the conference component.

It is advisable for the instructor to try to set time aside each week, during class sessions or during office hours, to meet with individual students regarding their progress in the course. The instructor should be prepared to discuss and to answer questions about those students' writing and grammar assignments.

It is especially advisable for the instructor to continually relay to the student what progress is being made, as well as updates as to where the student is with regard to course requirements. Use of the writing outcomes is extremely helpful in assessing student progress. These outcomes should be shared with students at the beginning of the semester.

COLLEGE COMPOSITION

Evaluation Sheet

Sentence Structure

    Subject/verb   _____

    Fragments   _____

    Run-ons   _____

Paragraphing

    Topic sentence   _____

    Support   _____

    Transitional phrases   _____

    Organization

        Time order   _____

        Space order   _____

        Order of importance   _____

Punctuation

    Commas   _____

    Periods   _____

    Apostrophes   _____

    Quotations   _____

Spelling   _____

Parts of Speech   _____

    Subject/verb agreement   _____

    Plurals   _____

    Pronoun agreement   _____

    Verb tense   _____

    Adjectives/adverbs   _____

Mini-Essay

    Introduction   _____

    Middle paragraph(s   _____

    Conclusion   _____

Essay

    Introduction

        Effective opening   _____

        Thesis statement   _____

        Preview   _____

    Middle paragraphs

        Topic sentences   _____

        Support   _____

    Conclusion   _____

COLLEGE COMPOSITION

Alternative Evaluation Sheet

Sentence Structure

    Subject/verb   _____

    Fragments   _____

    Run-ons   _____

Paragraphing

    Topic sentence   _____

    Support   _____

    Transitional phrases   _____

    Organization

        Time order   _____

        Space order   _____

        Order of importance   _____

Paragraph Types

    Description   _____

    Illustration   _____

    Comparison/contrast   _____

    Process   _____

    Persuasion   _____

Punctuation

    Commas   _____

    Periods   _____

    Apostrophes   _____

    Quotations   _____

Spelling   _____

Parts of Speech

    Subject/verb agreement   _____

    Plurals   _____

    Pronoun agreement   _____

    Verb tense   _____

    Adjectives/adverbs   _____

Dictionary Skills   _____

The BSA 025 Writing Portfolio

The BSA 025 writing portfolio is a collection of the semester's writing accomplishments. It gives you a forum in which to demonstrate your mastery of various writing techniques. The portfolio is an important part of your course grade (50%). This portfolio will provide an overview of your growth and development as a writer.

The BSA 025 writing portfolio must include *revised* copies of two of the three essays assigned during the semester—introduction, information, and persuasion. These copies must be typed or wordprocessed. The draft copies of these essays, with instructor comments and corrections, must also be included. The portfolio must contain four of your in-class writings, with instructor comments. (Although the choice of which writings to include is yours, the final in-class assignment from session 28 must be one of the writings included.) In addition, the research paper, as originally submitted, must also appear in your portfolio. The collection of writings must be introduced by a cover memo.

- The BSA 025 writing portfolio is to be placed in a three-prong *pocket* folder.

- All portfolios are due as indicated in your syllabus—session 30. No late portfolios will be accepted! There are no exceptions to this rule!

Cover Memo

The cover memo is your opportunity to evaluate your writing experience. You might, for example, discuss what writing strategies and techniques you have learned, what writing weaknesses you have overcome, what weaknesses you have yet to overcome, or what strengths you have discovered in your writing. This memo is an important part of your portfolio and should be crafted with great care.

BSA 025 WRITING PORTFOLIO CHECKLIST

Place a check by each item as it is completed and inserted into the portfolio. Please place the items in the order given.

_____ 1. Three-prong pocket folder

_____ 2. Portfolio checklist (to be placed in front pocket of folder)

_____ 3. Cover memo

_____ 4. First revised essay (introduction, information, or persuasion)

_____ 5. Draft copy of this essay (with instructor comments)

_____ 6. Second revised essay

_____ 7. Draft copy of this essay (with instructor comments)

_____ 8. Three in-class writings (unrevised, with instructor comments)

_____ 9. Final in-class writing (to be placed in back pocket of folder)

_____ 10. Research paper (to be placed in back pocket of folder)

— Important —
If you do not submit a writing portfolio, you will fail BSA 025!

_____
(Student signature)

_____
(Date)

3
Incorporating the Writing Process

The expanded coverage of journal writing is very good. I like the prompts *Evergreen* provides. It helps students discover themselves and their ideas, and they are more apt to do that if they feel that the journal writing doesn't have to be "ready for a grade."

Linda Whisnant, Guilford Technical Community College, NC

The journal coverage is excellent. Journal writing is important at the developmental level, and the additional information is well done.

Debra Anderson, Indian River Community College, FL

From Linda Whisnant, Guilford Technical Community College, NC

Write your own Invention Strategy Collection!

For this assignment, you will need some kind of timer such as a kitchen timer or a person who will watch a clock for you. Be honest! Do these samples according to the following time "rules." Otherwise, you won't get a feel for the technique.

In your notes, you will have written down five kinds of prewriting techniques, or invention strategies. You are going to produce a sample of each one for yourself. Do each of the numbered steps below on a separate sheet of paper. You may write on the back for this.

1. Set the timer for ten minutes. Freewrite "off the top of your head" whatever comes up for the ten minutes. This must not be less than a page and a half.

2. Set the timer for ten minutes. This time, first pick one of the following words. Write that word at the top of the page. Think about it for about ten seconds, and then start the timer. Write for the ten minutes about this concept, but if your thoughts wander, follow your thoughts as you write.

    RAIN DREAMS RED FIRST JOB COOKING STRESS

    I expect to see at least a page and a half for this one, too.

3. On the next sheet of paper, brainstorm about one of the following topics. You must come up with at least fifteen items. This is not a brain drizzle.

    My hobby   Planning a party   Favorite sport   A certain relative

    Your ideal room at home   Dieting   Reunions

4. On the next sheet, cluster. Choose one of the following topics. Again, make sure you have at least fifteen "bubbles," or circles with words.

    **Exercise   Heroes   Raising kids   Being a good employee   Music
    Teachers   Neighbors   Stress (if not chosen in exercise 2)**

5. Pick any topic on this page that you have not already chosen and write down at least eight questions about it. (Think of the typical "reporter's questions.") You are not supposed to try to write answers; just write questions that would give you more ideas on how to develop a paper.

Have this collection ready for me to flip through on _____.

From Susan R. McKnight, Tarrant County Junior College, TX

Promoting Student-Text Interaction

Whenever my developmental English students complete a reading assignment, they write one page in a double-entry journal. This learning tool helps them think about what they have read, relate to it personally, and reflect on how the material fits into the context of the whole course. While I use this exercise in English classes, it is a writing-across-the-curriculum strategy useful in any discipline.

The two parts of the journal are "What's It About?" and "What Does It Mean to Me?" Students may establish their own format. Some like to use the top half of the page for "What's It About?", in which they state three or four specific facts they consider most important in that reading. Below it, in the "What Does it Mean to Me?" section, they can respond in a number of ways to show evidence of critical thinking about the material. For example, they may choose to respond to questions such as these: How do I agree or disagree with the author's ideas? How can I apply what I learned to a new situation? If a problem is posed, are the solutions sensible? What new ideas occurred to me as I read? Another possible format, the side-by-side arrangement, allows students to respond directly to each of the main points of the lesson.

In addition to encouraging interaction with the text and critical thinking, the journals are an excellent tool for beginning class. I may start a discussion by simply requesting, "Take out your journals and tell us one significant point you gained from your reading for today." I know that even the most reluctant student has something to say and that he or she knows that at this point, any answer is correct because the response is whatever the student deems important, not a guess-what-the-instructor-has-in-mind answer.

Of course this academic journal can be modified to fit a specific assignment. Students can use it for short in-class writing assignments or add answers to the daily entry for a quiz. Sometimes I specifically request that "What Does It Mean to Me?" be completed in class, so that they can have some additional time between the reading and the rethinking. Since I often check journal entries during the first ten minutes of class, writing them encourages promptness as well as completeness. The original thinking reflected in them often serves as a starting point for writing essays. At the end of the semester, another advantage is that the completed journal is an excellent tool for reviewing the course.

Initially students may question the value of the journal, but generally after a few weeks they realize they are retaining more information and thinking about it in a new way. This assignment should never become humdrum. The number of ways the double-entry journal can be varied is limited only by the instructor's imagination.

From Keysha Ingram-Gamor, Montgomery College, MD

Emotional Scavenger Hunt

Students are to keep a journal for one week prior to the "Description" chapter. They should write about things that they experience during the course of the day, as in a diary. Students are told that they will use the material somehow the following week, but they are not given any more specific details or instructions. At some point during the chapter on description, students are instructed to go through this journal, searching for all their expressions of emotions, jotting them down as they progress through their record of the week. Whatever emotion is dominant will be the one they will use for their writing assignment. Now it's time to describe the abstract emotion that is dominant in their journal. Students share this emotion with the class, under the constraint of not using the actual word (or synonyms or antonyms for this emotion). The class will guess the emotion by listening to each description. This activity can be used competitively for an inexpensive prize, such as a can of a beverage or a vending machine snack or a piece of fruit. Students can simply use an ordinary sheet of paper for their scoring sheet. The teacher will be the host, reading each description, and the students will be the contestants.

From June J. McManus, San Antonio College, TX

Journal Assignments

When I assign a reading from *Evergreen* to be read before students come to class, they may choose to relate to it in some way in their journals immediately after reading. Then, at the beginning of class, I almost always assign a ten-minute journal entry relating to the reading. For example, when they read Richard Rodriguez, I may ask them to write about an experience they had on a summer job, or when I assign Martin Luther King, I may ask them to write about the absence or presence of racism on our campus.

Journal Assignment for English 301

Purpose of the Journal

To make the student more comfortable with writing, through using what he or she is learning or has learned or experienced as sources for creative thinking and essay writing.

Requirements

An 8 1/2 x 11" lightweight looseleaf notebook; title page with name, course, section. Minimum of five entries a week, dated. Circle the dates of two each week for me to read. Writing every day is beneficial. Varied entries, in-class writing and out-of-class writing. Students should bring journals to class every day.

Instructions

- Begin with a title page.

- Write for yourself. You are your audience.

- Write a summary of each assigned essay. Then comment in some way on the essay.

- You may write about any experience outside this class—television shows, newspaper articles, cartoons, movies, other classes.

- You will freewrite at the beginning of almost every class period. It is important that you bring your journal to class every day. These in-class entries are required.

- Read your choice of several unassigned essays from your textbook and respond to them. Many essays deal with science, nature, history, or other topics of interest to you. Look at the Rhetorical Index for the classification of subject matter.

(continued)

Journal Assignment for English 301 *(continued)*

Instructions *(continued)*

- Plan future educational experiences—reading, television, movies, museum visits, symphony concerts.

- Read over your journal occasionally. Comment on conclusions you can draw about yourself or your writing progress.

**• Avoid writing about your love life or personal problems unless they relate to this course.

- Keep a personal spelling list at the end of your journal. Add to it throughout the semester.

Grading

The journal will be taken up twice during the semester and then, finally, near the end of the semester. Each time I take the journal up, I will respond to two entries per week, but I will not mark mechanical errors. I will make suggestions and comments. Your final journal will be graded. This grade has the same value as the final exam. See your assignment sheet for due dates.

From Patricia Malinowski, Finger Lakes Community College, NY

Journals

An important part of the college composition course is encouraging the students to write often and at length. One of the most effective ways to accomplish this goal is through the weekly journal. This journal encourages the students to write both about themselves and about topical issues. It is suggested that the journal entry be of a specific length, such as two handwritten pages (both sides of a single sheet) or one computer-typed page. It is also suggested that journal writing be presented in a nonthreatening manner: that is, that it not be corrected for grammatical errors or graded. The journal can additionally be used to move the student from personal writing (subjective: Journal 1, Autobiographical) to academic writing (objective). Some suggested modes for inclusion are summary writing, letters to the editor, and letters of job application. Current research shows that the journal is effective in lowering writing anxiety and motivating students to express themselves freely at length. The journal should also serve as a means of making the instructor better acquainted with the student and as an unofficial record of the student's growth.

Samples

Journal Assignments Sheet

Journal Topic Sheets (A new topic sheet might be distributed at the beginning of each unit.)

JOURNAL ASSIGNMENTS

One journal entry (front and back of a sheet of standard note-book paper) is due each week. You should follow the schedule below.

Unit I
Journal 1 — Autobiographical
Journal 2 — Descriptive
Journal 3 — Topic Sheet Choice
Journal 4 — Free
Journal 5 — Topic Sheet Choice

Unit II
Journal 6 — Process
Journal 7 — Topic Sheet Choice
Journal 8 — Example
Journal 9 — Free
Journal 10 — Topic Sheet Choice

Unit III
Journal 11 — Topic Sheet Choice
Journal 12 — Comparison/Contrast
Journal 13 — Topic Sheet Choice
Journal 14 — Persuasive
Journal 15 — Free

1. Journals are due on the day stated on the class assignment sheet.

2. Please state at the top of your journal entry the topic you have selected.

3. Also state at the top what skill you are presently working on, for example, verb tense.

If you are unable to fill the space allotted to the assigned topic, complete the journal entry by writing about any topic you wish. There is no excuse for an incomplete journal entry!

Journal Topic Sheet 1

The journal topics for this unit will take a different direction from your previous assignments. In this unit, we hope to introduce you to some additional basic writing skills that you will use in your college career.

The journal topics for this unit will require more time, but you will be given specific assignments and directions for each. There will also be two assignments that will be completed on the computer.

The rules for journal assignments remain the same: if handwritten, a sheet front and back; if done on the computer, one sheet. Assignments are due on the day specified on the calendar.

The schedule for this unit is as follows:

Journal 11   —   Writing a summary

Journal 12   —   Comparison and contrast of ideas

Journal 13   —   Using other sources to support your opinion (persuasion)

Journal 14   —   More persuasion

Journal 15   —   Letter writing

It is important that you understand the requirements for each of the assignments. If you are not sure, ASK.

Examples

1. Give examples of pet peeves that you have.

2. Give examples of problems you face at home, school, or work. Explain these examples thoroughly.

3. Give examples of changes you would like to make in a product. You might consider a car, a TV, and so on.

Comparison/Contrast

4. Compare and contrast your parents' and your own attitudes toward some subjects. You might consider work, school, dating, marriage, and so on.

5. Compare and contrast how a favorite place looks during two different seasons.

6. Compare and contrast the experience of going out to a movie and watching a movie on TV.

Persuasive

7. Write a memo to your employer persuading him or her to change some aspect of your job or to give you a raise.

8. Write a letter to a close friend who has asked you for advice on a major decision he or she has to make. You might write about remaining in school, applying for a college internship, changing jobs, and so on.

9. Support or refute the idea that your high school years are the best time of your life.

10. Persuade me to buy a new car, a new vacuum cleaner, a . . . !

Journal Topic Sheet 2

Description

1. Describe career opportunities in your field.

2. Describe some childhood memories. What is your earliest?

3. Describe a local tourist attraction (e.g., a lake, an oceanfront beach, a gorge or mountain, a state park).

4. Describe a pet or other favorite animal.

5. Describe whom and what you would like to take with you on a very long space voyage.

Narrative

6. Describe an incident in which you were treated unfairly or felt cheated.

7. Write your own fantasy or science fiction tale.

8. Relate a humorous incident from your past.

Process

9. Explain one of the processes connected with your job (e.g., creating an ad, food preparation, cashing out customers).

10. Describe a familiar process (e.g., school registration, registering a car, taking a driving test).

11. Explain the steps involved in teaching someone to do something (e.g., ski, drive, quilt, crochet, weld).

Examples

12. Choose five of your positive qualities and give several examples to support your statement that you have them.

13. Give examples of some unfair laws. Why are they unfair?

14. Give examples that demonstrate that "experience is the best teacher' or that "you can't judge a book by its cover."

Comparison/Contrast

15. Compare and contrast high school and college.

16. Things seem to change as we grow older. Write about the changes in your feelings toward someone or something, from when you were a child to now.

17. Compare and contrast two cities or two vacation spots.

18. Compare and contrast two brands of something (e.g., two makes of cars, two brands of cereal).

Persuasive

19. Persuade me to purchase (or not to purchase) a certain item (e.g., a car, a VCR, a gun).

20. Persuade me to eat (or not to eat) at a fast-food place (e.g., McDonald's, Wendy's, Burger King).

21. Should teachers give exams? Write a convincing response.

22. Should spelling and grammar be considered in the scoring of an essay exam in a class other than English? Explain your view in a way that will attract others' support.

23. Should students have to take courses outside of their majors (e.g., English, mathematics, psychology, sociology, speech)?

Journal Topic Sheet 3

Descriptive

1. Describe a trip you have always dreamed of taking. You might consider Hawaii, Australia, and so on.

2. Imagine that you are employed by a nationally famous toymaker. You have been told to design a toy likely to become a national fad, such as the Cabbage Patch Kids. Describe the toy you would design.

3. Describe the fears and reservations you had at the beginning of the semester.

4. Describe an incident from which you learned an important lesson.

Narrative

5. Write an episode for your favorite television program.

6. Create a new ending for a book or a movie.

7. Relate a conversation you wish you could have with a famous person. Consider someone from either the past or the present.

Process

8. You are working for a large advertising company. Explain the process you would use to introduce a new product.

9. Describe the process you use to prepare a favorite meal or snack.

10. Describe the process you would use to help a new pet become a "member of the family."

Examples

11. Give examples of advertisements that are misleading to the consumer.

12. Give examples of cartoons or other children's TV shows that you feel should be taken off the air.

13. Give examples of some recent fads and explain why they were good or bad.

Comparison/Contrast

14. Compare and contrast two TV programs.

15. Compare and contrast two friends.

16. Compare and contrast the toys you had as a child with the "toys" you purchase for yourself now.

Persuasive

17. Select any recent controversial subject. Give your opinion and try to persuade the reader to agree with your side on the issue.

18. Should schools be allowed to test students for drugs? Develop a strong case, either for testing or for not testing.

19. Argue for the positive changes you would like to see made in your community, your college, or your local school system.

20. Should college athletes be required to take the same courses as other students to receive a degree, or should they be allowed to participate in a program designed especially for the athlete? Write a convincing affirmative answer to one of these questions.

Name _____

Journal 2

Describe the current state of your desk, your car, your kitchen, or your closet. In the left column, add some sensory details that a person in the class would need to fully picture the scene.

Freewrite:

Comments:

Do you have enough details?

Total earned: _____ /5

From Sandra K. Hall, Corning Community College, NY

Prewriting

Journal Sheets

- Journal entries, as a prewriting activity, allow a writer to di
Write freely.

- Grammar and spelling do not count.

- Journal sheets are due at the beginning of the first class of

- Journal entries give writers additional practice with a type

- Each journal entry should be a page long.

- Journal sheets are worth up to five points each.

- Late journal sheets will receive reduced points.

- You have been given a journal sheet for each week. If yo
room, staple a second sheet on top.

- Return journal sheets that I have seen to your folder; you
back of the sheet for a later journal entry.

Sample journal sheets follow.

Journal 3

Describe a person you know very well. Include physical details, behavior, and hints about personality. Your journal sheet will be sealed in a time capsule and read by a relative of this person in the year 2050.

Freewrite:

Comments:

Do you have enough details?

Would this interest the relative?

Total earned: _____ /5

Name _____

Journal 5

Explain in detail how to do one of these things: eat with chopsticks, iron a shirt, rollerblade, or get to an area landmark from campus.

Freewrite:

Comments:

Are the details clear for a beginner?

Have you given enough directions?

Total earned: _____ /5

Journal 7

Name _____

Write about examples of inexpensive recreation in your area OR movies or songs that contain too much violence OR social problems that concern you. Be sure to be descriptive.

Comments:

Freewrite:

Your audience is _____

Have you defined "inexpensive" or "violent"?

Do you have enough details?

Total earned: _____ /5

THE WRITING PROCESS:

Moving from Freewriting to Peer Review

Prewriting for Formal Paragraphs and Essays

Early in the assignment period:

- Review the appropriate chapter in the book.

- Do freewriting about a topic, on scrap paper.

- Read over the Planning Sheet for the assignment.

- Complete the Planning Sheet. Do not leave blanks.

- Hand in the Planning Sheet with the final draft.

At the writing stage:

- Write a rough draft from the Planning Sheet. At this point, worry about a topic sentence, organization, details, spelling, sentence structure, grammar, and so forth.

- Only now are you ready for the Peer Review class! (If you do not complete all these steps and bring a rough draft to class, you are considered UNPREPARED—which equals an ABSENCE!)

Planning Sheet for Paragraph 1

Describe an Object

Your topic:	**Your Attitude:**
An unnamed object	It is "useful" or _____

Brainstorm and freewrite for ten minutes on this topic. Include as many physical characteristics and sensory details as would help identify it. (These include size, dimension, composition, chips in the paint, etc.)

- Now look at the object again, from another angle. Are there any details you have overlooked?

- What seems to be the most important part of the object—the part that you really want to focus on?

- Assume that your AUDIENCE is

    an eleven-year-old who is wired to a Walkman playing heavy metal music and whom you have asked to go and get this object

- Now that you have identified your audience, what does this person need to know about the object?

- What is your PURPOSE in sharing this paragraph with your audience?

    _____ To get that person to find it?

    _____ To get that person to care about that object?

    Other: _____ _____

Moving into the Writing Stage with Paragraph 1

Now, on your *own paper,* write your first draft. Write on one side of the paper and skip lines. **Remember:** A planning sheet is *not a rough draft*!!!!!

Checklist Before Peer Reviewing

✔ Pay close attention to the topic sentence (<u>underline</u> or *highlight* it).

✔ Does it immediately grab one's attention?

✔ Does it introduce a limited topic and attitude toward the topic?

✔ Do you deliver (in the paragraph) what you promised in the topic sentence? (How will the eleven-year-old and your peer who reviews the paragraph be able to tell your can opener (e.g.) from the other can openers on the table?)

✔ Have you arranged these details in a space order that a reader can follow? (See *Evergreen,* pp. 47–50.) When you describe the object, do you jump all around or move in a logical spatial order?

✔ Insert transitional words to help this audience follow you— words such as the following. (See *Evergreen,* p. 60.)

> *next to, near, close to, on top, beneath, left,*
> *right center, front, back*

✔ Does the paragraph have an appropriate closing sentence?

✔ Make some beginning revisions as you read it over.

　Should you add or take out any details or transitional words?

　Should you change the order of any details?

✔ Proofread for errors that you detect.

✔ At the top of the rough draft, write a title that *predicts* your topic and attitude.

You are now ready for the Peer Review!

Peer Review—Description: Paragraph 1

Writer's name: _____ *Reader:* _____

Topic: _____

Title: _____

---

1. Underline the **topic sentence.** Is it limited enough?

2. Does the opening grab your attention? Why or why not?

---

3. Who is the **audience?**

_____

(Is it a general audience or a specific one, such as a family member?)

---

4. What is the central impression being conveyed? (What is the writer trying to communicate?)

---

5. Put a wavy line under any vague words. Discuss with the writer ways to be more *specific.*

Prewriting/Planning: Paragraph 3—Process

How to . . .

(See *Evergreen*, pp. 92–101, for help.)

Topic: How to _____

Purpose: To explain a process clearly

Attitude: This process is _____(easy, important, etc.).

Audience: _____

Criteria: Steps must be in chronological order; topic sentence must contain a conjunctive adverb; final draft must be done on a computer

BRAINSTORM

Order

✔ Number the steps in chronological order.

✔ Remember your specific audience: Have you included all the steps and details he or she needs to follow your explanation?

Rough Draft

On your own paper, write your rough draft. Skip lines.

✔ <u>Underline</u> your topic sentence and make sure it has a **conjunctive adverb.**

Example: "It is difficult to iron a shirt; **however,** you must follow these steps."

✔ **Proofread** for errors, especially the ones you tend to repeat. (Check your list of strengths and weaknesses.)

✔ Include **transitional words** like *first, next,* and *finally* (p. 96).

✔ Make sure you have an encouraging **summary sentence.**

✔ Test your paragraph on a friend: Ask the friend to pretend he or she has never eaten spaghetti (e.g.) and to follow your steps in his or her mind. Does the friend get lost or confused at all? *If yes, revise.*

✔ Ask the friend, "Have I made the process clear and interesting? Have I used description to help you follow me? Have I been specific?"

✔ Add a **title** that reveals your topic and purpose.

You are now ready for the Peer Review!

Peer Review: Paragraph 3—Process

Writer: _____   *Reader:* _____

Topic: How to _____

Title: _____

Is it specific? Does it state that the paragraph will explain *how to do something?*

Purpose: To explain a process clearly

Attitude: This process is _____(easy, important, etc.).

Audience: _____

Criteria: Steps must be in chronological order; topic sentence must contain a conjunctive adverb; final draft must be done on a computer

---

Topic Sentence

✔ Underline the topic sentence.

✔ Circle the conjunctive adverb and check for correct punctuation.

Example: "It is easy to rollerblade; **however,** you must take certain precautions."

Order

✔ Number the steps in chronological order.

✔ Has the writer included all the steps and details you need to follow the explanation?

✔ Are the instructions **specific** and **detailed?** (Be alert for vague words like *thing* and *thingamajig.)*

✔ Has the writer included transitional expressions like *first, next,* and *finally?* (p. 96)

✔ Has the writer made the process clear and interesting?

Planning Sheet for Paragraph 5—Examples

(See *Evergreen,* pp. 67–75)
Final draft must be done on computer and saved!

Topic: To explain, by providing three descriptive examples, the term you defined in Paragraph 4.

Topic: _____

Purpose: To explain by examples.

Attitude: These examples are important, to clearly explain:

(Without my examples, some people might confuse stress with panic, etc.).

*Audience:*_____

(It helps to imagine your audience as a person in the commons who is struggling with this concept to prepare for a test. How can your examples help?)

Criteria: 1. Make sure each example is clear and descriptive.

2. Make sure all examples are relevant.

3. Arrange them in order from least important to most important.

4. Include at least one *complex* sentence. Underline it.

Brainstorm: At least ten minutes on your topic. Generate as many examples as you can, then toss out the weaker ones.

Order

✔ Examine the order of your ideas.

✔ Remember your specific audience.

✔ Have you included all the details and examples your audience needs to follow your explanation?

Moving to the Writing Stage

Rough Draft

On your own paper, write your rough draft. Skip lines.

✔ <u>Underline</u> your topic sentence.

✔ Proofread for errors, especially the ones you tend to repeat.

✔ Make sure you have one **complex sentence.** <u>Underline</u> it.

✔ Include **transitions.**

✔ Make sure you have a satisfying **concluding sentence.**

✔ Test your examples on a friend. Are they clear enough?

✔ Ask a friend to describe the tone of your paragraph:

_____

(humorous, helpful, serious, sarcastic, sentimental, . . .

✔ Add a title that reveals your topic *and* purpose.

Poor example:	A Race Car Fan
Better example:	How to Spot a Racing Car Fanatic

You are now ready for the Peer Review!

Planning Sheet for Essay 1—Comparison or Contrast

(Refer to pages 115–131 for additional help.)

General Topic

Compare or contrast yourself to the way you were five years ago.

Freewrite here about yourself then and now. Include similarities and differences:

Analyze your freewrite.

- <u>Underline</u> points that interest you.

- Can you **categorize** them (for example, changes in appearance, changes in interests)?

- Now decide which you want to focus on: similarities or differences.

- Now, select only the most significant, most interesting similarities or differences and arrange them in two lists.

List A: Five years ago   **List B:** Now

Topic

PURPOSE (Am I primarily writing a COMPARISON or a CONTRAST?):

AUDIENCE (Who might read this with interest 25–50 years from now?)

What is the POINT of my comparison or contrast?

Organization

Have I arranged a clear BLOCK pattern of **four** paragraphs?

Have I used clear **transitions,** such as *in contrast, but, however, on the other hand, in addition, similarly?*

Do I set up a clear order within paragraphs 2 and 3 (see p. 184–189)?

Outline for Essay 1

Title: _____

INTRODUCTION—Paragraph 1
THESIS   (Appears at end of Paragraph 1)

BODY—Paragraph 2   5–7 Sentences Long
TOPIC SENTENCE Point 1 Point 2 Point 3   Are your points in the best order?

BODY—Paragraph 3   5–7 Sentences Long

TOPIC SENTENCE
 	
Point 1
Point 2
Point 3
    Are your points in the best order?
    Do you follow the same order as in Pararaph 2?

CONCLUSION
     What has been the point of your comparison or contrast?

You are now ready for the Peer Review!

Planning Sheet: Persuasion by Cause and Effect

EXIT ESSAY

Read Chapter 13, pp. 150–165.

SUGGESTED TOPICS

Because of these reasons (effects), high school sports should be eliminated.

Colleges should require computer literacy courses because of these benefits.

Steuben County's Workfare Program should be ended (or continued) because the program is having these effects.

_____ Your own topic; get it approved by me.

TOPIC

Select one of the above, alter it to suit your values, or get another topic approved by me.

_____

Am I arguing for or against? _____

Can *reasonable people* argue the opposite point of view?

Is my topic limited and manageable?

Have I picked a more "middle of the road" position, rather than an extreme one?

AUDIENCE Read page 154 carefully!

Identify a *specific* audience (such as a person thinking about going to college who does not have any computer skills).

My audience is _____

This audience also contains 20 people who *strongly disagree* with your position. Describe these people in positive or neutral terms, not negative ones.

(continued on next page)

THE FIVE BASIC METHODS OF PERSUASION   pp. 153–154
Use these to support your thesis.

FACTS (What facts can you include? Remember to identify all outside sources!)

1.

2.

3.

Use only *very specific facts*. Do NOT say, "**A lot** of kids are injured every year in team sports, and **many more** lose self-esteem because they weren't picked for the team."

REFERENCE TO AN AUTHORITY

According to _____, _____

EXAMPLES (For instance, how did you feel playing an intense game of basket-ball, or how did a friend feel starting college without computer skills?)

1.

2.

(Examples, too, need to be **specific and descriptive**).

Do not say, "**Some** of my friends came to college without computer skills and . . .

Say, "My friend Chris ended up in a freshman English class that required computer skills. She spent 20 hours the first week begging for help in the lab, lost two nights of sleep, and chewed Tums by the handful."

As with *any borrowed information, identify sources* that are not from personal experience.

PREDICTING THE CONSEQUENCES (What might happen—positively and neg-atively—e.g., if sports remain fiercely competitive?)

ANSWER THE OPPOSITION   CONCESSION

Be reasonable here; do not use button pushers like "our kids will grow up to be wimps if we eliminate football."

Show that you are aware of the opponent's argument, but . . .

(Example: People who are opposed to competitiveness in high school sports are not losers or wimps, but are people seriously concerned about injuries, academics, and good sportsmanship).

(continued)

List their reasons and concerns.

How will you answer their reasonable concerns?

TONE   Your tone must be reasonable.

Avoid name calling and button-pushers.

Avoid extreme positions (such as no sports).

Avoid *you* if at all possible—it puts an audience on the defensive: "If you are in favor of competitive high school sports, you don't care about all the kids injured each year."

THESIS

✔ Take a clear position in your thesis. Use *should* if possible.

✔ LIST, here and in your thesis, the three *reasons* you have identified as the best ones to support your position.

   1.

   2.

   3.

✔ Arrange these reasons in order from **least** to **most important.**

✔ Mention them *in your thesis in the same order* in which you plan to cover them in the essay.

   Example: "I agree that safety, academics, and good sportsmanship are important, but there are valid reasons for maintaining a high school sports program."

(continued)

INTRODUCTION

Part I: Lead off with several sentences that introduce your topic.

Part II: State what the opposition believes is important. (Concession)

Part III: Answer the opposition with your thesis:

Thesis: _____

_____

Make sure you identify your reasons in your thesis.

PLAN FOR SECOND PARAGRAPH—REASON NUMBER 1

Notes to yourself here. What methods of support can you include?

PLAN FOR THIRD PARAGRAPH—REASON NUMBER 2

What methods of support can you include?

PLAN FOR FOURTH PARAGRAPH—REASON NUMBER 3

Notes to Yourself

This should be your most important reason.

What methods of support can you include?

What emotional appeals can you fairly include (such as the thrill of victory or pride in doing one's best?

TRANSITIONS (See p. 152.)

CONCLUSION Fifth Paragraph (probably)

✔   Sum up your reasons.

✔   Make a final point.

Do not introduce a new topic such as:

"Teens who are very competitive in school sports go on to be very competitive in life and work."

(If you haven't covered this as a reason, do not throw it in at the end!)

From Sherrie H. Lynch, Andrew College, GA

A Supplemental Exercise for Chapter 1: Writing for Audience

As a supplement to Chapter 1, I add an exercise that students keep in their journals. To reinforce the significance of keeping audience in mind while writing, I ask students to write about events at a recent party, in three separate journal entries: for themselves, for their parents, and for their classmates. Students feel comfortable and are expressive when writing an entry for themselves because I tell them that this entry is "for your eyes only" and that I will not collect it as a part of the journal assignment. After they have written all three entries, I ask volunteers to read the entries for classmates so that they can get immediate feedback from their audience. Finally, we discuss the general differences among the entries, pointing out important concepts such as diction, formality, and appropriateness.

A Supplemental Activity for Chapter 23: A Revising Strategy

After the class reviews Chapter 23 as an introduction to revising, I put the students to work revising their own essays, using the skills highlighted in the chapter. However, I do expand the process somewhat.

First, the students pair off. (They should work with a different partner each time.) Each pair finds a quiet place—an empty classroom, a corner in the hallway, or a bench outside—where each partner will read his or her paper to the other. In doing so, the students can listen for rhythms, determining whether sentences have a variety of structures and lengths. In addition, they can check immediately for surface errors. After an essay is read, the students discuss content concerns: clear thesis, organization, adequate development, unity, and coherence. Following the oral reading and discussion, the partners trade papers and each silently reads the other's paper. Students write in the margins of the essay, pointing out strengths and weaknesses as they see them. Not only are students honing revising skills, they, as readers, are helping the writers focus on the audience's needs and concerns. When students get their papers back with comments and suggestions, they become aware of the back-and-forth work involved in the revising process, and they learn they must decide what revisions they will incorporate in their papers.

From Ann Longknife, College of San Mateo, CA

Writing Process

Students come to us unsure of their ability and often dismayed at finding out how much they do "wrong." In teaching at the developmental level, I have found it extremely important to focus on what they can do and, even more important, to help them see how far they have come. I find the layout of *Evergreen: A Guide to Writing* very helpful.

In the first full class period, I carefully go over Chapter 1, asking questions to make sure the students understand the concepts of subject, audience, and purpose. Then I assign a paragraph, using Practice 4, prompt 2. First I ask them to list all the things—both physical and social—they have noticed about the college. Then I ask them to write a short essay to fulfill the assignment, first explaining that this is just a practice and not a graded assignment. I also tell them to come and ask me about any spelling or grammar problem. If they know enough to ask, they are already on their way to learning more. I read the essays and make a general comment, pointing out strengths and weaknesses. I also let the students read the essays and then return them to me.

The next classes are spent on a combination of writing and grammar assignments, using the writing chapters in *Evergreen* and parts of the basic grammar section. Students' original essays give me information about where I need to place the greatest grammar emphasis.

A month later I pass out their original essays to let them see what corrections they can make to improve them, and I assign a rewrite. Often my students are amazed at how badly they wrote before and take pride in being able to improve their first efforts so markedly. Again, I am available to answer any questions.

Then, after another month has passed—just before the midterm—I have them do another evaluation and rewrite. This time they discover a lot of things they want to do differently. I grade this effort and it becomes one of the grades for the class. Seldom does anyone get less than a B, and that reinforces the message I've tried to make clear—with work and with study, an effort that is not so good can be made much better.

The important outcome of this assignment, made much easier by the way *Evergreen* is set up, is that students discover that they *can* improve their performance and learn *how* they can do it. Then, they know that the decision as to how much time and effort they want to put into their projects is up to them.

From Cliff Gardner, Augusta College, GA

Showing Students How to Revise to Improve Content Development

Supplementary Exercise for Chapter 23 *"Putting Your Revision Skills to Work"*

Rationale for Exercise

Many students find that their writing instructors encourage them to improve the development of their ideas in the body paragraphs of their essays as they revise. This exercise attempts to help students do two things: (1) begin seeing opportunities for elaboration and illustration in paragraphs that have relatively weak development and (2) act on those opportunities by adding specific illustrations and descriptive details to paragraphs.

Writing Sample A

As you read the following paragraph, notice that each of the underlined sentences is a generalization—a sentence that states a point in general terms. There is nothing wrong with the statements made; the problem is that these points may not register in the reader's mind with as much impact as they could with good follow-up examples or descriptive details.

My bedroom is my favorite room in my house because it is a place of freedom for me. To some people, having their own bedroom is no big deal. For me, though, it is a privilege because I had to share a room with my older brother for eighteen years. Now that he has moved out, I have a chance to put my own personal mark on the room. While my parents chose to furnish the rest of the house with country decor, I have decided to go with more modern furniture. I've also replaced the pictures on the walls. And now that my brother is gone, I can do whatever I want without being concerned about another person. My bedroom is not just a place where I sleep; it is a place where I make the choices.

Now read the revised version of the paragraph. Notice the examples and descriptive details added after each underlined sentence to bring each general point to life.

My bedroom is my favorite room in my house because it is a place of freedom for me. To some people, having their own bedroom is no big deal. For me, though, it is a privilege because I had to share a room with my older brother for eighteen years. Now that he has moved out, I have a chance to put my own personal mark on the room. While my parents chose to furnish

(continued)

the rest of the house with country decor, I have decided to go with more modern furniture. I now have a matte black entertainment center for my stereo, and a formica drawing table instead of my childhood desk. My room is highlighted by matching cylindrical table and floor lamps that have glass discs mounted on top. I've also replaced the pictures on the walls. In place of the familiar old landscapes I grew up with, I've hung a wide assortment of framed posters and photographs of people. Now I'm surrounded by a gallery of faces, from the Black Crowes to Courtney Love to a street person from San Francisco. And with my brother gone, I can do whatever I want without bothering another person. I sleep when I want, have private telephone conversations anytime I want, and play Nine-Inch Nails with the volume dial set at 8. My bedroom is not just a place where I sleep; it is a place where I make the choices.

Writing Sample B

Step 1: As you read the following paragraph, underline any sentences that you think might be elaborated on in order to add life or emphasis to them. Look for any sentence that makes a point in a general way; imagine how you might bring the statement to life with effective illustration(s) and descriptive details.

Without a doubt, the waiting room of a doctor's office can be one of the most uncomfortable places in the world. Oh, the seating is not really uncomfortable. However, the chairs are too close together. What makes a waiting room most uncomfortable is being cooped up with strangers who are sick. Also, it's bad enough to run the risk of catching all those different diseases, but when there are badly behaved children sitting across from you, it's hard on the nerves. And the wait seems to go on forever.

Step 2: Now rewrite the paragraph, adding examples and descriptive details after each sentence you underlined above. Remember the purpose of this exercise: **to add life to generalizations in writing by including sharply focused, specific illustrations and descriptions.**

Writing Sample C

In essays, the easiest method of improving content development is to "beef up" the body paragraphs. Read the following essay and follow the same two-step pattern used previously: (1) underline in the body paragraphs all the sentences you think might be brought to life with added support; (2) then rewrite the essay, adding sharply focused specific examples and descriptive details after each sentence you underlined.

Make the essay come alive for a reader. With each addition, try to add **impact** and **vividness** to the generalization you are supporting.

Different people have different notions of what constitutes a perfect weekend, of course. As for me, I feel satisfied with my weekends when I've done three important things. Early in the weekend, I like to get the small chores and errands that need to be done out of the way. Another "must" activity for me during any weekend is getting a good physical workout. Most important of all, I need recreation, typically with one or more of my friends.

Before I let myself relax and enter the "fun mode" on Saturday, I always take care of household jobs and run any necessary errands. Every week I have laundry and apartment cleaning to do. Often I listen to music while I clean to make these tasks seem less tedious. I typically go to the grocery store next to get the week's shopping done. Unlike many other people, I enjoy grocery shopping. Sometimes I stop at other stores while I'm out to get more things I need. I try to finish all my chores and errands by midafternoon.

After half a day of such duties on Saturday, I want to do something that will get my muscles moving, my heart pumping, and my mind cleared. Exercising fits the bill perfectly. I usually do either of two things: go to the gym or get in a long run. Afterward, I feel a wonderful sense of relaxation.

By Saturday evening, I'm ready for recreation. Often I have a date, but some Saturday nights I go out with a friend or a group of friends. Usually we eat out and catch a movie, although occasionally we spend the evening at one of our apartments. I find that I just don't feel right about a weekend unless I wake up Sunday morning with memories of fun from the night before. On Sunday afternoons, I sometimes like to do some socializing as well.

I use my weekends to get a little work done and to relax. After a good weekend, I feel recharged and ready to meet the world again on Monday morning.

Additional Exercise: Revising One of Your Own Essays

Of course, the focus of the writing course is improving your own writing. When you are writing your own original essays, keep this principle in mind: As you write, look for opportunities to follow up general statements with effective examples and descriptive details. Well-chosen illustrations and details plant ideas more effectively in a reader's mind.

As an exercise, select one of the essays you've already written this term and revise it by:

(1) Rereading the body paragraphs and underlining any sentences that present ideas in a general fashion only

(2) Rewriting the essay, adding effective examples and descriptive details to enhance your presentation of each idea you underlined

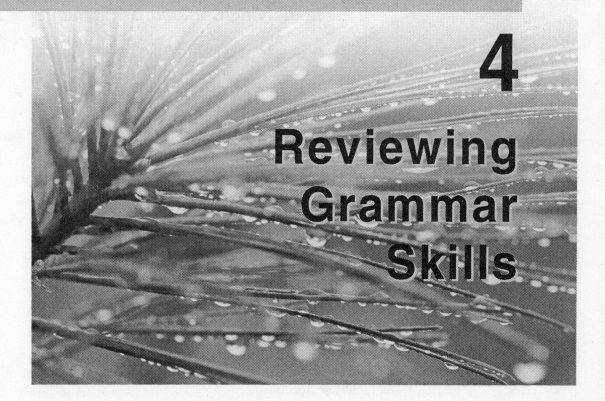

4
Reviewing Grammar Skills

I have used *Evergreen* longer than any other college text. It provides an excellent balance of instructional material for all areas of emphasis. The layout is very user-friendly for both students and instructors. This is a classic among English composition texts.

Debra O. Callen, Harold Washington College, IL

Evergreen probably has the best treatment of sentence-combining skills available for the beginning writers in English composition courses. *Nobody* doesn't like *Evergreen!*

Michael Douglas, Savanna State College, GA

From Kathleen Beauchene, Community College of Rhode Island, RI

Identifying/Correcting Fragments

Assignment: Use this practice to correspond with Evergreen, 7th Edition, Chapter 26.
 Note: Evergreen doesn't mention the "detail" fragment, but it is a common type of fragment, so I have added it here.

Directions: Read each numbered item below. If it is correct, put a C. If a fragment exists, do the following:

(1) Underline it.

(2) Label the type of fragment you have found. Fragment types include:
 Dependent clause (*because, since if, as, although, . . .*)
 Relative clause (*who, which, that, whom*)
 -ing modifiers
 Prepositional phrase (*in, by, with, from . . .*)
 Infinitives (*to* plus a verb)
 Detail (*for example, for instance*)
 Appositive

(3) Correct the fragment by adding what is missing or by connecting it to a complete sentence.

_____ 1.   With Christmas coming soon. I will need to save some money.

_____ 2.   Rhode Island drivers have the worst habits. For example, never using their blinkers.

_____ 3.   Registering early ensures that students get a good schedule. Because most courses close by the first week.

_____ 4.   I hate some household chores more than others. Like cleaning bathrooms.

_____ 5.   When I heard the results of the presidential election, I was in shock.

_____ 6.   Being an excellent artist. John decided to attend an exclusive art school.

_____ 7.   My son bought one of those scooters. That all the kids have now.

_____ 8.   One way to check for fragments to read each sentence out loud.

_____ 9.   To succeed in college, you need to review material frequently.

_____10. My family loves to get together. Especially at Thanksgiving.

_____11. Although I used my coupons. I still spent too much money.

_____12. Karen played the slot machines. As if her life depended on winning.

_____13. Most students are anxious for the semester break. Studying can be a chore.

_____14. An energetic child. Samantha did not sit still at any point during the parade.

_____15. Since you don't know the trails well. I will lead our group on the mountain bike expedition.

From Kathleen Beauchene, Community College of Rhode Island, RI

RO/CS Practice

Assignment: Use this assignment to correspond with *Evergreen* 7th Edition, Chapter 26, pages 358–373.

Directions: Use Chapter 25, Part E to help you complete this assignment.

(1) In the space provided on the **left,** write RO beside run-on sentences, write CS beside comma splice sentences, and write C beside sentences that are punctuated correctly.

(2) Then correct each error by using any of the five methods summarized in Chapter 25. In the space on the **right,** write the number of the method you've used.

RO, CS, or C   **Method**

_____ 1. My computer has been helpful in doing school work writing papers is a breeze now. _____

_____ 2. My boyfriend constantly sends me emails, but I have deleted most of them. _____

_____ 3. Many drivers are rude, last night someone hit my parked car. _____

_____ 4. This semester I am overwhelmed, my English class keeps me especially busy. _____

_____ 5. *Lord of the Rings* is a popular book now it is also a popular movie. _____

_____ 6. Sara was the best runner on the track team, she won many awards for the season. _____

_____ 7. Registering for classes is confusing students often find that the classes they need are closed. _____

_____ 8. My gym offers a variety of programs, but my favorite is using free weights. _____

_____ 9. The concert began people rushed to find their seats. _____

_____ 10. Learning about run-on sentences and comma splices is easier than I thought some of my classmates are still confused. _____

From Ray Foster, Scottsdale Community College, AZ

Practice with Complex and Compound Sentences

I have taught developmental English classes using the *Evergreen* texts for several years.

I find Chapter 25, "Coordination and Subordination," in *Evergreen* most helpful in getting students to understand correct sentence structure with its accompanying punctuation. To emphasize the chapter's importance, I have devised the following activity:

> Each student is to bring to class three compound sentences taken from ANY page in the *Evergreen* text. They are also asked to bring three sentences from the text that are complex sentences.

> Each student is asked to write one sentence from each category on the board. The student discusses how each compound sentence can be made into a complex one, and then he or she explains how to turn the complex into a compound (or simple) sentence.

The entire activity is time intensive, and, though every student is asked to bring sentences, not all students are able to make individual presentations. I am able to get through about six students per class.

Students enjoy the break from traditional lecturing, and the basic ideas of coordination/subordination appear to have more significance.

From Ray Foster, Scottsdale Community College, AZ

Regular and Irregular Verbs

If time permits, I use the lists of the three principal parts of regular and irregular verbs (Chapters 27 to 29) to have students quiz each other before any class lecture. I have a student turn to the student next to him and give that student ANY one of the three parts of the verb. The "quizzed" must then give the other two parts of the verb. This is a very successful use of verbally "hearing" the verb's correct principal parts "in action."

From Linda Whisnant, Guilford Technical Community College, NC

Identifying Groups of Words

In the blank, write **I** if the group of words is an independent clause, **D** if it is a dependent clause, or **P** if it is a phrase of some kind (there are several kinds of phrases).

<u>**Think:**</u> What do you **have to know** about a group of words to label it correctly? In class, we think together and come up with the two questions you need to answer in order to identify a group of words:

(1) Does this group of words contain a verb and a subject?

(2) Is this group of words a complete *thought?*

_____   1. After lunch, my family is leaving to go to Myrtle Beach

_____   2. Although she had done all of the homework assignments

_____   3. Running down the road with a rock in my shoe

_____   4. Until John receives an offer of employment

_____   5. Until last year, Jack and Carol lived in San Diego

_____   6. Until the arrival of the cargo plane from Puerto Rico

_____   7. Life in America seems more complicated these days

_____   8. Life with all its mysteries to ponder

_____   9. That man over there is staring strangely out the window

_____   10. That he might find happiness in his marriage

_____   11. As soon as the semester is completed

_____   12. Which class did he take during summer school

_____   13. Which lasted for over three months

_____   14. How lovely she looks in her wedding dress

_____   15. How he did that with one hand behind his back

_____   16. How he did that with one hand I will never understand

_____   17. Down the street marched the band

72 **Chapter 4**

_____ 18. Calling every twenty minutes to try and reach her

_____ 19. That dog just barked

_____ 20. Whomever you contact will be glad to help you

Copyright © Houghton Mifflin Company. All rights reserved.

Chapter 32: Prepositions
(Practice Review, pp. 433–434)

The essay concerning Dr. Daniel Hale Williams provides an opportunity to experiment with more than just preposition errors. What I do is take the same essay format and create additional errors, in consistency and parallelism, wordiness, and capitalization. The students have to identify the errors and then rewrite the entire essay. This exercise reinforces accurate proofreading skills as well as grammatical structure and style. My version of the same exercise follows.

Grammar

Directions: Identify the following errors in capitalization, exact language, conciseness, consistency, parallelism, and variety in sentence structure. Rewrite the essay in its corrected version. Proofread carefully for accuracy. (20 pts.)

Dr. Daniel Hale Williams, Pioneer Surgeon

In a lifetime of many successes, dr. Daniel Hale Williams' most greatest achievement was to pioneer open-heart surgery.

young Williams, An african american who grow up in the mid-1800s, knew Poverty. He relied on his wits to get by, becoming, in turn, a shoemaker, then a Musician, and then a barber. At the age of twenty-two, he met Dr. Henry Palmer, who soon see he was capable of becoming a physician. Williams' education, the usual one at the time, in the medical field consisted of a two-year apprenticeship with Dr. Palmer, followed by three years at the Chicago Medical College, where he is specializing in surgery.

It was a good time in medicine science. Surgeons had just started using antiseptics in order to protect and prevent patients against infection. "Dr. Dan," as he was now called, became an experienced expert in the new surgical techniques. "Dr. Dan" became a leader in Chicago's medical and Chicago's African-american communities. In 1891, he succeeds in opening Provident Hospital, the first interracial hospital in the United States for all races. There, African Americans were assured first-rate, top-of-the-line medical care and taken care of. Moreover, black interns and nurses received thorough and complete professional training.

It was to Provident Hospital that frightened friends brought James Cornish on the evening of July 9,1893. Near death, the young man had received a deep knife gash near his heart during

---

a fight. Dr. Williams decided to operate immediately since he was sensitive to the dangerous situation. According to eyewitnesses, he first made a six-inch incision and removing Cornish's fifth rib. Then, he repaired a torn artery and stitched up the punctured sac surrounding the heart. Fifty-one days later, Cornish left the Hospital, recovered and deeply grateful to Dr. Williams for his life. The age of open-heart surgery had begun.

Much lay ahead for Dr. Williams. He was responsible for reorganizing the Freedmen's hospital at Howard University from 1894 to 1898; in 1913, he accepted an invitation from the american college of surgeons and succeeding in becoming its only African-American charter member. The high point of his life, however, remained that night in 1893.

From Patricia Malinowski, Finger Lakes Commity Gollege, NY

Grammar Component

For the grammar component, the student could be assigned one or two individual chapters of each unit in *Evergreen* or from a supplemental text such as *Grassroots*. The assignment of these chapters should be based on the instructor's assessment of the student's weaknesses in writing and grammar. The evaluation of these deficiencies can be continuous during each unit, and the instructor should be ready to supplement weak areas.

The student should be instructed to work through each chapter that has been assigned. Depending on the instructor's preference, the student should self-correct the chapter either section by section or in its entirety. At the conclusion of the chapter, the student should inform the instructor that he or she is ready for a chapter test. Some instructors prefer to confer briefly with the student and check the text responses.

Instructors may wish to specify two chapter-test days per unit and note these on the student calendar. This will enable students to plan and study for these tests and not wait until the last week of a unit to hurriedly complete grammar chapters.

An instructor may decide to handle this grammar component with either whole-class or group/collaborative activities. No matter which strategy is employed, it is important that class and individual study time be used to instruct students in correct grammar usage.

Chapter tests are provide by the publishers of *Evergreen*. These tests are available in the test packet, and there are at least two chapter tests for each grammar chapter.

Instructors should set a specific grade for students to attain for each chapter. A suggested grade for mastery is 80% or better.

From Russ Gaudio, Gateway Community College, CT

What Are My Options?

The options chart (p. 353) illustrating the process of combining sentences in Chapter 25 of *Evergreen: A Guide to Writing,* "Coordination and Subordination," serves as an efficacious teaching tool for instructors of developmental writing and as a visually clear reference guide for basic writing students.

Preparations

I clearly define and illustrate what a clause is, the difference between one that is independent and one that is dependent, and the role of coordinating and subordinating conjunctions (pp. 343–357). I then have students redefine terms, so as to correctly interpret the options chart: the adjectives *coordinate* ("of equal rank or importance") and *subordinate* ("placed in or belonging to a lower order or rank"), and the noun *option* ("the act of making a choice or exercising a preference").

Co	=	equal, with, together
Sub	=	under, beneath (dependent)
Ordinate	=	to put in the same rank or order; to match
Options	=	choices (variety in joining simple sentences and determining relationships between them)

Coordination

Here I engage the class in a *T*eacher–question and *C*lass–answer session on coordination, using the chart (p. 353).

T: What does the box on the left say for Option 1?

C: Independent clause!

T: On the right?

C: Independent clause!

T: If the clause on the left is independent and the clause on the right is independent, what are they?

T/C: Equal and coordinate!

T: What is the process of joining them called?

T/C: Coordination!

We chant the same choral dialogue for Option 2 and Option 3, following the graphic layout that clearly delineates the concepts under study. Since I find that many students (1) place a comma *after* the coordinating conjunction when joining sentences and (2) become generally "baffy" over comma usage in general, I established the "comma so bafy" rule for Option 1—so that students will remember to place a comma BEFORE *so, b (but)*, and *a (and)* and before an *f (for, or, nor)* or *y (yet)* when choosing a coordinating conjunction to establish a relationship between independent clauses.

I help students to easily memorize the first three options by looking at the chart and answering my questions as indicated (it is a given that an independent clause sits on either side of the option).

T:	Option 1?
C:	Comma so bafy.
T:	Option 2?
C:	Semicolon.
T:	Option 3?
C:	KEEP the semicolon; ADD a conjunctive adverb FOLLOWED by a comma.

Subordination

Now I initiate the next *T*eacher-question and *C*lass-answer "vocal," still following our chart (p. 353).

T:	What does the box on the left of Option 4 say?
C:	Independent clause!
T:	What does the box on the right of Option 4 say?
C:	Dependent clause!
T:	If the clause on the left is independent and the one on the right dependent, what are they?
C:	Unequal. One is dependent on the other!
T:	What is the process of joining them called?
T/C:	Subordination!

We reiterate the same choral rhythms for Option 5 and then begin to review (it is a given here that a subordinating conjunction introduces the dependent clause).

T:	Option 4?
C:	Independent clause!
T:	Followed by?
C:	Dependent clause!
T:	With?
C:	No punctuation!
T:	Option 5?
C.	Dependent clause!

T:	Followed by?
C:	Comma!
T:	Followed by?
C:	Independent clause!

At this point I initiate another question-answer mode for all the options, using fill-in-the-blank types of questions (along with, I confess, Victor Borge punctuation gestures and sounds), saying the answers in unison with the students. It is purposeful pantomime of sights and sounds and gestures.

T:	Option 1
C:	Comma so bafy.
T:	Option 2
C:	Semicolon.
T:	Option 3 Keep the—
C:	Semicolon. Add a—
C:	Conjunctive adverb. Followed by a—
C:	Comma.

The class enjoys my dog-and-pony show antics but at the same time learns the options. I then cajole the students to volunteer (almost everyone eventually "wants into" this act) and recite the chart from memory as I roam up and down the aisles asking for options in rapid-fire fashion.

End Results

Finally, students are required to keep a copy of the options chart in a writing folder as an ongoing reference for all remaining writing assignments and class exercises; in this manner, they learn to familiarize themselves with the coordinating and subordinating conjunctions as well as with the conjunctive adverbs. More important, students now have the opportunity to practice, apply, and grasp the serious and powerful mechanisms of coordination and subordination, to add variety to their expression, and to gain a sense of style.

From Ann Longknife, College of San Mateo, CA

How Words Work

One of the techniques I have used is to take the readings—or at least a paragraph or two—and have the students change them—perhaps put everything in past tense, use all past participles, or make contractions where none exist. Another technique I have used very successfully, to show how words work and how important changing a word can be, is to have them take a paragraph and find another word for the verb or adverb or adjective. They may use a thesaurus, but they still need to be sure the new word does approximately the same thing the old word does.

After they have changed the words, I have the students put a couple of sentences on the board and we discuss which choice was best and why. This gives them the exercise of finding the new word, seeing what new words others have chosen, and examining how each of these word changes has altered what is being said. They really begin to see what a difference even a subtle change or a slightly different word can make.

From Ann L. Lathrop, Lehman College, NY

Grammar and Mechanics

In the first two weeks at the beginning of the semester, before a more detailed review, I give an overview of the parts of speech and sentence functions (subject, object, subject complement, verb or predicate, etc.) so that the students and I have a common metalanguage with which to discuss their writing and the explicit grammar lessons that will follow. I then use the chapters on grammatical structures and mechanics (Chapters 24–37) as a general review for the class and on an as-needed basis for students experiencing difficulty with specific structures. ESL students also need supplementary work concerning articles, modals, gerunds, infinitives, and prepositions.

5
Writing Paragraphs and Essays

The balance between paragraph development and composing short essays in *Evergreen* allows instructors to tailor this text to their individual methods of teaching composition. I emphasize entire essays. Other instructors place more emphasis on practice with individual paragraph construction. Instructors who design composition courses with widely divergent emphases find the text eminently satisfying.

John Thornburg, San Jacinto College, TX

I think the balance of paragraph/short essay writing is well designed. Since the authors provide lists of possible topics for writing in each strategy, the instructor can easily decide on the number of assignments appropriate to the capability of any particular class: sometimes emphasizing paragraphs, at other times spending more time on essays.

Muriel M. Brennan, College of San Mateo, CA

From Joseph Fly, South Plains College, TX

How Do You Start This Thing?

A strange space ship has crashed outside of town. We believe that the following paragraph is a correct translation of the start-up manual, but the statements are not in the right order. Your task is to figure out the correct order, and rewrite them in a short list, numbered 1 to 6. Keep your list as simple as possible by deciding what information you will need and leaving out any unnecessary details. Good luck, and let's try not to blow this one up.

Turn on engine exhaust ports only after the power is on. Increase antimatter influx mix after the main power is on. The viewing screen will not operate unless all control panels have been activated. Never fire the main thrusters without the viewing screen on. If you activate the control panels before you increase the antimatter influx mix, you will burn out all the dilithium crystals; that is a bad thing. Turn on the engine exhaust ports only just before firing the main thrusters. The main power must be on for anything else to function.

Answers for How Do You Start This Thing?

1. Turn main power on.

2. Increase antimatter influx mix.

3. Activate all control panels.

4. Turn on viewing screen.

5. Turn on engine exhaust ports.

6. Fire main thrusters—lift off!

From Kathleen Beauchene, Community College of Rhode Island, RI

Essay Form

This assignment corresponds with *Evergreen*, Chapters 14 and 16. It can also be used with "The Illustration Essay" on pages 198–201.

Having the door closed on me one too many times led to the following assignment, which I call "How Rude!"

1. After I relayed my experience of people ignoring me as I, with books, bags, and assorted teaching instruments in hand, wrestled to open a door to the corridor, students began to share their various rude encounters. We then concluded, "Rude people are everywhere." With this idea in mind, we brainstorm different environments where people exhibit their rudeness: school, sporting events, movies, roads, grocery stores, malls at Christmas time, and so on. I then divide the class into groups based on four or so of the listed locations.

2. For homework, each student then brainstorms examples of rudeness in his or her assigned location. During the next class session, students gather in their designated groups. For example, students in the "movie" group share their examples and come up with a group brainstorm. For homework, each student then writes his or her paragraph and saves it to a disk.

3. When we return to class, I ask each student to copy his or her paragraph onto my disk. (I teach in a computerized classroom, so this process is easy for me. In a traditional room, a laptop would work just as well.) Through our campus computer system, I email all students and attach the file that contains the paragraphs. In my email, I ask students to select two paragraphs—each on a location that is not the one they were assigned—and to save them to their disks. (I remind them that they should select paragraphs that are similar to their paragraph in tone. If they have written a serious paragraph, they probably don't want to select a humorous one.) They will then have three paragraphs that will eventually comprise the body paragraphs of an essay. I also ask them to bold their own paragraph. Students return to class with a hard copy of the paragraphs.

4. We work on creating a thesis that effectively unites the body paragraphs. Each student is responsible for creating his or her own thesis but can use those suggested by the class. With that thesis in mind, students decide on the best way to arrange their body paragraphs. They then review each paragraph to:
    a. Ensure that has a topic sentence.
    b. Add appropriate connecting devices.

c. Make grammatical corrections and ensure that the body paragraphs are similar in voice and point of view. If there are inconsistencies, students need to make the appropriate revisions.

5. Once they feel comfortable with their body paragraphs, we review Chapter 16, "The Introduction, the Conclusion, and the Title." We explore various methods of beginning an essay. To illustrate "begin with a direct quotation," I share with them an article I found on "Rudeness," and they select a quote to use to open their essay.

6. Finally, they create a conclusion.

7. Students then complete their essays and come to class with a hard copy to share with their group.

This assignment occurs over three or four class sessions, but it is a worthwhile vehicle to teach essay concepts. Students have the support of their groups and are able to take each step slowly.

From Kathleen Beauchene, Community College of Rhode Island, RI

Recognizing the Essay Form

This assignment corresponds with *Evergreen*, Chapter 14.

Organizing an essay is problematic for many of my developmental writing students. For that reason I spend some time reviewing and practicing the form before assigning an essay. Two activities have proven to be helpful in illustrating the essay form.

1. Because we approach the essay format after working on the paragraph form, I find that the easiest way to present the essay form is by initially linking it to the familiar paragraph form. We begin by reviewing the essay material in *Evergreen*, Chapter 14, on pages 169–197. Students then take a past paragraph and enlarge it to fit the essay form as illustrated on page 170. I re-create the form to make the assignment easier for them.

2. We review the essay form in the text on pages 169–170 so that students become familiar with identifying a thesis, finding connecting devices and topic sentences, and recognizing the special characteristics of an introduction and conclusion. I then find an essay in the text, such as "Libraries of the Future—Now" on pages 199–200. I arbitrarily label each paragraph with a letter of the alphabet, make copies, cut up the essay on the basis of paragraph formation, scramble the paragraphs, and paper clip together. (If I am teaching this class in our computerized writing classroom, I scan the essay and then label and move the paragraphs around. Using our campus email system, I send the essay as an attachment and proceed as explained below.)

3. In class, I give students the paper clipped paragraphs and ask them to use their knowledge of the essay format to guide them as they unscramble the essay. After about fifteen minutes, I begin to circulate the room and provide appropriate hints. If students continue to have problems after my intervention, I then allow them work in small groups where they help each other.

4. When they think that they have put the essay into the appropriate form, I have them compare their version with the original. Their comparisons then form the basis for class discussion that revolves around the essay form. For example, if a student has the introduction as the last paragraph, our discussion might focus on thesis placement or introductory versus concluding techniques. If a student has placed what should be body paragraph 2 in the body paragraph 1 position, we might look at each paragraph to identify the topic sentence or connecting devices, such as transitional words, to determine if the writer provided clues regarding paragraph placement. We might also look at the relationship of each body paragraph to the thesis. In other words, would one body paragraph follow more logically from the thesis? Did the thesis provide an explicit hint, via a preview statement?

From Kathleen Beauchene, Community College of Rhode Island, RI

Practice with Titles

The assignment that appears on the next page corresponds with *Evergreen,* 7th Edition, Chapter 16, Part C, "The Title."

I find that many students omit titles, write lackluster ones that do not invite readers in, or include a hastily conceived title—one that is usually quite general in nature.

After discussing different aspects of the title as presented in Chapter 16, I present students with a multiple-choice activity to test whether they can link a movie title with its description. I have intentionally stayed away from the most recent movies, which would be familiar to most students. To update the listing, I merely cut and then add in another title and description. While I obtain these descriptions from a local paper, similar descriptions can be found on www.blockbuster.com or on other video/DVD rental sites. Another option is to use classic movies rather than current ones.

I encourage students to try the activity on their own first and then allow for small group work. We use this activity as a vehicle for a "title" discussion that revolves around obvious titles, play-on-word titles, straightforward titles, and humorous titles. Of course, I point out downright bad titles, often evidenced in any TV Movie of the Week. We also discuss how titles should match the tone of a movie, essay, or book.

As a follow-up activity, I take an essay that we haven't read, copy it, cut out the title, and ask students to provide a title for the essay. We then compare theirs with the original. Students are often impressed when their title is similar to the original or even better than the original.

A "Title" Exercise

Directions: Read the following movie reviews that appeared in the *Providence Journal* and match them to the titles.

The Descriptions

_____ 1. 40-year-old son moves back in with his mother to discover the essence of their relationship.

_____ 2. Charming, if predictable clash-of-cultures romantic comedy about a couple who get married, then find they don't know one another.

_____ 3. Sicko burrows into the life of her glamorous roommate.

_____ 4. Two feuding ex-presidents take to the road to save their lives.

_____ 5. White mob terrorizes a tiny black Florida town in 1923.

_____ 6. Rescue worker tries to save people trapped in an auto tunnel under the Hudson River.

_____ 7. Prodigy pianist tries to get out from under the thumb of his father.

_____ 8. Burglar witnesses a murder involving the president and is on the run.

_____ 9. Someone is killing the kids at Woodsboro High.

_____ 10. Mother fears the gloomy old mansion she's living in is also home a sinister presence.

_____ 11. Beauty school teacher goes to work for a dictator and tames him.

_____ 12. Town is in peril when a mountain erupts.

_____ 13. Lonely divorcee finds herself attracted to an elevator operator and learns to laugh and love again.

_____ 14. The first white man trained in the secret arts of the Japanese masters travels to Beverly Hills to save a beautiful woman.

_____ 15. Wives seek revenge of their ex-husbands with funny consequences.

_____ 16. Man tries to save his wife from violent truckers.

_____ 17. Toilet jokes galore in this look at King Arthur and the Knights of the Round Table.

_____ 18. A musical horror spoof about a couple in the clutches of a transvestite from the galaxy of Transylvania.

_____ 19. Long-divorced couple rekindles their flame, though now married to others.

_____ 20. Down-and-out gambler agrees to coach an inner-city baseball team and discovers his destiny.

The Titles

A. *ABSOLUTE POWER*

B. *THE OTHERS*

C. *THE BEAUTICIAN AND THE BEAST*

D. *BEVERLY HILLS NINJA*

E. *ROCKY HORROR PICTURE SHOW*

F. *DANTE'S PEAK*

G. *DAYLIGHT*

H. *MONTY PYTHON AND THE HOLY GRAIL*

I. *THE FIRST WIVES CLUB*

J. *LIVING OUT LOUD*

K. *BREAKDOWN*

L. *MOTHER*

M. *MY FELLOW AMERICANS*

N. *HARDBALL*

O. *THAT OLD FEELING*

P. *ROSEWOOD*

Q. *SCREAM*

R. *SINGLE WHITE FEMALE*

S. *SHINE*

T. *FOOLS RUSH IN*

From Kathleen Beauchene, Community College of Rhode Island, RI

"Picture This"

This assignment corresponds with Chapter 4 (pp. 44–65) in *Evergreen,* 7th Edition. At the time this assignment is given, students have not yet written an essay. I use this two-paragraph assignment as a precursor to the essay.

Select a photograph that has special significance to you. That photograph will become the basis of a two-paragraph assignment. (Do not select a portrait or picture taken at a photo studio.) Here's what you are going to do.

Paragraph 1

- Provide a general opening sentence to link your two paragraphs. In that sentence you might want to state what your photograph is about and perhaps when it was taken, as in "The photograph of my uncle is especially memorable."

- Using space order, describe who and what is in the photograph. You can use your book to review some space order transitions, such as *to the right, above, below, ...*

Paragraph 2

- Provide a topic sentence regarding the significance of your photograph. Using order of importance, present and discuss your reasons for the photograph's significance. If you have only one reason, then you might want to order your examples or details using order of importance.

- Provide an ending sentence for your two paragraphs.

From Robert Mann, Urban Campus, Des Moines Area Community, IA

The Party: A Variety of Exercises

Here is one exercise I have invented that works in a number of ways. This exercise may be applied to the following *Evergreen* chapters.

Chapter 1, "Exploring the Writing Process" (Subject, Audience, and Purpose, especially)

Chapter 5, "Illustration"

Chapter 6, "Narration"

Chapter 7, "Description"

Chapter 8, "Process"

Background for the students:

"Imagine there has been a big party on your block. There are cars parked everywhere. The music is really loud. There are people wandering over lawns neighboring the party house. The police are called by one of the neighbors. The police arrive. Arguments pop up. Some people are arrested."

Assignment: For Chapter 1, instructor to students:

"I am going to divide you into groups. You are to pretend you are one of the people at the scene of this party. Group A will be partygoers. Group B will be neighbors. Group C will be police. Now the police arrive. Let's start this scene. What would you most likely be saying, neighbors?"

After the role playing, lead a discussion of differences in viewpoints and presentations of the scene in all possible varieties: vocabulary, selection of detail, order of presentation of support, and so on, that are logically possible. What differences in purpose would the groups at this scene have and how would they be likely to demonstrate them? What are the differences in audience these groups would interpret and, again, how would these differences be shown? List these differences in some fashion on the chalkboard, as an example, so that students get an idea of interrelatedness, language, and organization.

Assignment: For Chapters 5 to 8, instructor to student, *re* this same scenario:

"Write a _____ (narrative, process, etc.) paragraph of the scene, pretending you are a police officer or a neighbor or a party goer. Write to (mother, friend, fulfill requirements of reporting). How does your choice of_____ (formality/informality, word choice, etc.) vary?"

From Ann L. Lathrop, Lehman College, NY

A Follow-up Lesson:
Chapter 3, Parts D, E, and F

To prepare students for expanding their writing from paragraphs into essays, I often use the song "Trash" recorded by The Bobs as a follow-up lesson to Chapter 3, Parts D, E, and F (pp. 32–42). Students enjoy the change of pace and medium, and ESL students especially appreciate having a script of the lyrics to refer to after they have tried to catch the main idea and the meaning after the first playing. The topic, messiness, is humorously appealing and easily recalls the earlier lesson involving the evidence of Pete's sloppiness.

The stanza form illustrates paragraphing and linkage to a basic theme or main idea. Each stanza begins with a reference to an adage (the topic sentence), develops that theme using lexical collocations (castle—royalty, queen; heart—cardiac arrest, care; godliness—heathen, heretic, altar, collection plate), and has a conclusion. The overall conclusion presents an extreme solution to the problem, but one that the listener has been prepared for. The lack of an introduction is a good point for discussion, and students working in small groups can try to write an appropriate opening. The instructor can also point out dialect (the use of the double negative: "I can't get no rest") and orthographic ("gonna") register differences if the students do not question their use.

Students talk with great animation about the irksome habits of roommates or spouses, and these discussions provide the basis for especially lively essays. Other related successful writing assignments involve strategies for getting rid of an unwanted roommate, the proper behavior for keeping peace with one's roommate, or proverbs from students' home cultures that students can apply to a central theme and fully develop with translations and explanations of the context in which they are uttered, their purposes, and their effects—all of which build on the model of the original paragraph from the textbook or the lyrics of the song and lead students easily toward full-length and well-formed essays.

From Sandra K. Hall, Corning Community College, NY

Moving from a Paragraph to an Essay:
Evergreen, pp. 169–172

To understand the difference between the paragraph and essay, I augment pp. 169–172 of *Evergreen* with this material.

Acting to Save Mother Earth

Every day we hear more bad news about our planet. What can we do in the face of such widespread gloom? **We can each learn practical ways to better our environment.** For example, saving and recycling newspapers has a number of positive results. Another Earth-saving habit is "precycling" waste. Wise management of hazardous household waste is yet another way of taking action for the planet. These personal actions may not seem important, but if carried out on a larger scale, they could greatly improve our environment and our lives.

The above paragraph contains three examples (circled) and uses transitions. Nevertheless, what problems do you see with trying to cover the topic in one paragraph?

Writing Exercises: Transitions

To help students understand the role of transitions in writing, I sometimes take an editorial from the *New York Times,* photocopy it, and cut it into paragraphs (and, where instructive, smaller meaningful units). I give each student an envelope with the "puzzle pieces" and require that the article be reassembled. In addition to demonstrating the importance of transitions in logical coherence, this project also enhances the students' sense of essay organization by forcing them to distinguish the likely opening paragraph(s), thesis statement, development, and conclusion. This exercise can be made increasingly challenging over the semester by, for example, picking an editorial with its thesis stated at the end, or an editorial where the thesis must be inferred.

From Susan VanSchuyver, Oklahoma City Community College, OK

Descriptive Writing

Resources

Chapter 7, "Description"
Chapter 22, "Revising for Language Awareness"

Type of Activity

Introductory group activity

Objectives

To introduce word choice, audience, and descriptive language
To promote creativity in the use of language

Directions

1. Decide how many small groups you will need to divide the class into groups of three to four students. Assemble at least five different colors of lipstick, markers, or crayons, and white paper. Draw a thick slash of each color on each sheet of paper and number each slash. Make enough pages that each small group has a page with five numbered slashes of color.

2. As a total group, discuss well-known and overused descriptive phrases used for colors: *fire-engine red, lemon yellow, sky blue.* Discuss the need to appeal to the senses and to interest the audience.

3. Give each group one of the sheets of paper with the five slashes of color. Tell the students that they must create a name for each color with a word or phrase that would make a customer want to purchase that lipstick or marker or crayon. Introduce the idea of appealing to the specific audience (customer).

4. After the groups have had time to name their colors (10–15 minutes), write the names on the marker board or use an overhead projector. First write down the names of the number one color from each group. Compare and discuss. Point out truly creative word choices. Continue for color two and so on.

Outcomes

Students will have a better understanding of audience; they will have a foundation for beginning to write descriptive paragraphs (Chapter 7) and essays (Chapter 15).

From Keysha Ingram-Gamor, Montgomery College, MD

Description, Comparison, and
Process Assignments

Description

I try to encourage the use of all senses in this unit. To achieve that, I usually conduct an activity that I call "Sense Stations: Painting Pictures with Words."

Before setting up the sense stations, I give a talk about the importance of description in any writing for any purpose. We discuss two ways of describing, objectively and subjectively. I have been surprised by how well the students understand how to distinguish between the objective description and the subjective description. Students generally do a fantastic job of deciding when and why each approach is appropriate. After analyzing the effects of figurative language in our readings and class activities, students are excited about painting their own pictures with words. I have found, too, that students love to explore their use of figurative language during this project. They are usually eager to share their stories. In my experience, this activity has proven to be one that students enjoy and remember.

I set up in the classroom stations or sections wherein the use of one sense is dominant. A station for each of the five senses is crucial, and I leave instructions at each station so that students will know what is expected. I encourage (require) each student to take notes as the observation is occurring, for these details will suffice as information gathering. When the student's two-minute visit is up, he or she will write a brief paragraph describing the experience. In the end, the students will write a story using all the details they experienced while visiting each station. Having students who are unable to experience a particular station—the auditory station, for example—proves to be a valuable lesson for the entire class regarding the importance of a variety of approaches or appeals. Some station suggestions:

Try to help students have a variety of stories they could create. Students need only to complete the paragraphs of the stations they plan to use in their stories, but it's crucial that they gather information at all stations.

Many times students are unfamiliar with the station names. Teachers are presented with an opportunity to work in some key root words.

I. Ocular
   A. Collage—allows personal experience to dictate what the student sees
   B. Picture—of an object, a historical figure, a place, or whatever you like
   C. Object

II. Auditory
   A. Sounds one hears at night in the country or city
   B. Different types of music
   C. Sounds heard during different weather situations

III. Olfactory
   A. Sweet—perfume or flowers
   B. Foul—chemical, animal, or other
   C. Nature—seasonal associations; i.e., evergreens evoking thoughts of winter

IV. Tactile
   A. Sand or sandpaper
   B. Wet (something wet or something cold or warm)
   C. Brittle—dry leaves
   D. Squishy—dough or cooked noodles

V. Palatal
   A. Salty
   B. Sweet
   C. Bitter
   D. Spicy (whatever you choose—try to target every part of the tongue)

Comparison and Contrast

1. *Let's Make a Deal!*
   I have students compare their two textbooks for class Their goal is to convince me to discontinue assigning material from one of the texts. If they are successful at writing thoughtful statements indicating pros and cons of each text, in the end—supporting their choice—I will give them a break from homework taken from that textbook, for some predetermined period.

2. I assign students to write a paper explaining why this paper is going to be better (not repeating the same errors) than the last one.

Process

1. I have students analyze three articles on the same subject, in an effort to study fact and opinion, then write a paper about how they approached this analysis.

2. I write different locations, all on campus, on a piece of paper and tear the paper into pieces so that one location is on each sliver. Students select a piece out of a bowl. Their task is to give someone directions from the designated point on campus to their classroom. They cannot forgo context—explaining the purpose, indicating an audience, and so on. Students really enjoy this one. They should be encouraged to go out and walk through the process, taking notes along the way. This assignment can be completed as an in-class writing assignment.

From Angela L. Chilton, Tarrant County Junior College, Northwest Campus, TX

Developing Persuasive Essays

One of the biggest writing problems our remedial students face is development; this refers not to methods of using the facts in their knowledge base but to their having a very limited knowledge base concerning local, state, national, and world issues.

To remedy this shortcoming, I requested from our Houghton Mifflin representative videotapes usually reserved for history, government, psychology, and sociology. In class, our writing students receive a persuasive writing prompt and we collaboratively brainstorm for examples. This session usually results in students' being able to state their opinions but unable to support them, due to lack of examples and specifics. Responding to this need immediately, we watch a video on a related topic and take notes. When we finish the videotape, we again collaboratively list examples, augmenting our previous list with real and specific details. The students then have much more information and a greater opportunity to write a passing essay. At the next class meeting, the students write an in-class essay using that information; they do not use their notes (since the TASP test, for which they are preparing, allows no such reference materials). With this plan, they incorporate the information into their knowledge base and exercise their memories.

With this method, our students overcome knowledge deficits, one topic at a time. They also comment that writing is much easier when they know what to say. This encourages them to become more aware by watching or listening to news programs and reading more newspapers and news magazines. Students become more alert to issues and often see opportunities to become involved in the issues we cover in class. They also develop a respect for the need and benefit of research as a part of the writing process. Here are some sample video programs and writing prompts.

Prompt

Should the federal government regulate the environmental impact of businesses? Proponents believe that businesses will damage the environment with toxic waste unless the government imposes and enforces safe standards. Opponents believe that businesses should regulate themselves without further federal interference.

Your assignment is to write an essay, 300–600 words, to be read by a classroom instructor, in which you support one side of this argument. Be sure to use appropriate reasons and examples to defend your stance.

Related Video

The Environmental Protection Agency. Illustrates the various forms of pollution, their causes, and the creation of the Environmental Protection Agency.

Prompt

Who should be the ultimate authority for interpreting the U.S. Constitution: the Supreme Court or a majority vote of U.S. citizens? Some believe that Supreme Court justices are more knowledgeable and experienced in matters of constitutional rights. Others believe that the Supreme Court is too political, basing decisions primarily on Republican and Democratic platforms.

Your assignment is to write an essay, 300–600 words, to be read by a classroom instructor, in which you support one side of this argument. Be sure to use appropriate reasons and examples to defend your stance.

Related Video

The Supreme Court. Details the Webster Case, illustrating the division on the abortion issue between Supreme Court decisions and state regulations.

Chapter 14
"The Process of Writing an Essay"

Based on the essay composition section, I provide an *outline* for the students to follow with all of their essays. This assists them in organizing their ideas, understanding connections between ideas, and condensing information into a main idea/subpoint format. Indeed, this outline parallels the structure of all the essays in Chapter 15, "Types of Essays." It further illustrates how essays, despite diversity in type, (narrative, descriptive, classification, comparison and contrast), still adhere to the same structural foundation in composition.

Title

Thesis Statement (Central idea in *one* sentence only)

I.   Introduction
   A. Attention getter
   B. Thesis statement introduced

II. Body
   A. Main idea (topic sentence)
     1. Subpoint
       a.
       b.
     2. Subpoint
       a.
       b.
   B. Main idea (topic sentence)
     1. Subpoint
       a.
       b.
     2. Subpoint
       a.
       b.
   C. Main idea (topic sentence)
     1. Subpoint
       a.
       b.
     2. Subpoint
       a.
       b.

III. Conclusion
   A. Summary
   B. Concluding statement

From Anne Richey, Interboro Institute, NY

Lesson Plan
Evergreen, Chapter 13
"Persuasion"

Introducing Persuasion

To introduce persuasion and to make argumentative writing seem less daunting to my students, I often begin with a hypothetical case or situation that requires the students to provide solid evidence that could be used to support our chosen position. This discussion *precedes* our examination of Chapter 13. I keep the issue noncontroversial so that our deliberations stay on track; we are marshaling evidence, not debating the issue. I write my students' suggestions on the board. Usually they come up with facts, examples, predictions, authorities, and sometimes answers to the opposition. With the occasional less imaginative class, I prompt them. Once we have ten to twelve very specific points on the board, I note the types of evidence discussed on pp. 153–154 in Chapter 13, write them on the board, and then ask the students to classify their ideas according to those types. They are always pleasantly surprised to see they're already adept at using argumentative evidence. "This," I say, "is not something I have to teach you, for you do it in your daily lives every time you have an argument or discuss an important issue. My job," I continue, "is to help you be more aware of the methods of support you use and to point out their strengths and pitfalls." From there we get into detailed discussion of argumentation. When I assign their essays, I require students to use at least three types of evidence and to label them in the margin.

Chapter 13, "Persuasion," as a Basis for the Research Paper

This semester, I am trying a new approach to term paper writing. I am requiring that my English 101 students base their research papers on an argumentative essay. This approach, I hope, will enable students to see that research has a practical application and that it can not only buttress a presentation but also enlarge it. My plan is to have them write their required persuasive essay, choosing from a list of fifteen topics that I know inspire strong opinions and whose treatment does not require much more than common sense and experience, at least in this first stage. Once the essays are graded, I will require that the students use them as the foundation of their research papers. At this point, they will be expected to begin their research, looking for facts, examples, predictions, authorities, and statistics that they can integrate into their essays to make them more convincing. Along the way, I will guide them on the use of bibliography cards, note taking, library use, documentation, and so forth. When I collect the papers, I will keep my fingers crossed that this time I'll be reading work that reflects conviction, some real footwork, and the students' voices.

6
Suggested Writing Topics

The discussion and writing questions following each reading are exceptionally well done. They impressed me as thoughtful and engaging. They do an exceptionally good job of separating the questions into "levels," with the questions for discussion involving recall and moving to some analysis, and the writing assignments inviting students to synthesize and be creative.

Linda Whisnant, Guilford Community Technical College, NC

Evergreen's strongest plus for me has been the writing assignments based on photographs, and those at the end of each reading. They inspire creativity and evoke students' interest in one another's responses; class members become willing, even eager, to read their papers aloud. Lively discussions ensue.

Margaret Koenig, Monterey Peninsula College, CA

100

From Joseph Fly, South Plains College, TX

Sensory Details Exercise

Using specific sensory details, describe the following locations:

1. An old barn

2. A new-car showroom

3. The inside of an igloo

4. A dog kennel

5. A hospital operating room

From Sherrie H. Lynch, Andrew College, GA

Specific Writing Assignments from *Evergreen*

1. Describe a room in your home. Describe one that is special to you—the bedroom, the kitchen, or the den. Choose details that capture that special feeling of the room. Be sure to organize the details in space order before you begin to write the rough draft.

2. Describe the photograph I have provided you, as clearly as you can. First, jot down several important details in the scene. Then arrange these details in some sort of space order. Do this prewriting before you begin your rough draft.

3. Study the photographs that I gave you of the two couples. Look carefully at their facial features and expressions, at their body language, at their clothing, and at their surroundings. Compare and contrast the two couples. First, jot down the similarities and differences you see. Ask yourself a few questions: What is my general impression of each pair? How do they seem to be getting along? How are the couples alike and how are they different? Do your prewriting before you begin your rough draft.

From Patricia Malinowski, Finger Lakes Community College, NY

Evaluation Assignments

Unit I — Evaluation

Write a clear and well-developed paragraph on one of the following topics. Remember to narrow the topic, write the topic sentence, brainstorm, and select and arrange your ideas before you write your rough draft and your final draft. HAND IN ALL WORK.

1. At some time, we have all accomplished something either at work or at school that we are proud of. Describe an accomplishment you are proud to have achieved.

2. We often find ourselves in the wrong place at the wrong time or saying the wrong thing. This leads to embarrassing situations. Describe an embarrassing incident in your life.

3. People are an important influence in our lives. Describe several ways in which someone has influenced your life. Remember that influences can be positive or negative.

Unit II — Evaluation

Select ONE of the following topics and develop it into a mini-essay. Make sure you have an introduction, a middle paragraph (or paragraphs), and a conclusion. You should hand in all your work: brainstorming, organization, rough draft, and final draft.

Topics

1. Illustration (examples)—People who have overcome handicaps, poverty, prejudice, and so on

2. Descriptive—The effects of a rainstorm or snowstorm

3. Narrative—An experience in which you were embarrassed or disappointed

4. Cause and effect—Why so many young students are afraid of school

---

Unit III — Evaluation Essay

Write an essay of four or more paragraphs on one of the following topics. Include an outline, first draft, and final draft.

1. Describe the things that you would change in your community and why.

2. You are one of the last people of your generation on earth. Select three items that you would leave for future generations. Defend your choices.

3. The law has made the use of seat belts mandatory in the state of New York. Do you agree or disagree with the law?

4. Does television serve a purpose or is it just the "boob tube"? Explain your opinion.

Unit III — Alternative Evaluation Essay

Select one of the following topics. Write an essay in which you give an affirmative or a negative response to the question. Your essay should consist of an introduction in which you have a clear thesis statement, at least three paragraphs that support your thesis, and a conclusion.

1. Should there be mandatory testing for AIDS?

2. Should people with AIDS be allowed in the workplace? To attend school?

3. Should people who knowingly transmit AIDS be liable to criminal prosecution?

4. Should health care professionals (doctors, nurses, lab technicians) have the right to refuse to work with AIDS patients?

5. Should the government (local, state, or federal) sponsor programs in which clean needles are given to drug addicts in exchange for old needles?

6. Should a hospital be held liable if a patient contracts AIDS during a hospital stay or from a blood transfusion?

From Jane Wilson, Ivy Tech State College, IN

Paragraph Writing Assignments

Chapters 5 to 13 on paragraph styles provide rich opportunities for in-class writing assignments. These writing assignments change from semester to semester; the listing below is only a sample of topics used.

1. **Illustration**

   What is your favorite TV show, and why? Use examples.

   How do you successfully study for a test? Use examples.

2. **Narration**

   (Please see p. 6.)

3. **Description**

   You have just heard Thoreau's description of Walden Pond. Describe the area for me in your own words.

   Describe the car of the future, as you see it.

   Describe your favorite place. Invoke all the sensory images that apply.

   Describe a specific table in the classroom in such detail that I will be able to find it among all the others.

4. **Process**

   Tell me how to accomplish a task you know well; pay particular attention to including all necessary details and steps.

5. **Comparison/Contrast**

   Read these short biographical sketches of two individuals and compare and/or contrast them.

For the comparison/contrast writing assignments, I provide the biographical sketches, in my own words, and we discuss possible criteria for evaluation. I also bring in samples of my own or student writing on various topics and ask the students to analyze them.

From Anne Richey, Interboro Institute, NY

Argumentative Essay/Research Paper Topics

1. Day care—Effects on children

2. Television violence—Effects on children/viewers in general

3. Exercise—Its importance for mental and physical health

4. Abortion—Parental permission for teens

5. Gangsta rap—Images of women reflected in it

6. Teenage suicide—Causes

7. Organ transplants—Who gets them and when

8. Crash helmets for motorcyclists—Mandatory or not?

9. Doctor-assisted suicide—Legal or not?

10. College athletes—Exploited by their schools?

11. Automation—Should there be limits when jobs are at stake?

12. Animals—Do they have feelings?

13. Ultra-thin models—Effects on young girls' self-images

14. Juvenile delinquency—Should parents be the ones who are punished?

15. Athletes—Steroid use

From Susan McKnight, Tarrant County Junior College, TX

Sample TASP Writing Assignments

Assignment 2(a)

Are professional athletes paid too much? Some people feel that athletes are paid too much, receiving multimillion dollar contracts just for playing a game. Others feel that the huge salaries players receive are only their fair share of the billions of dollars the owners receive from concessions and television rights.

Your purpose is to write a multiple-paragraph essay, between 300 and 600 words, to be read by a group of National Football League owners. You take a position on whether professional athletes are overpaid. Be sure to defend your position with logical arguments and appropriate examples.

Assignment 2(b)

Should the United States prison system abolish parole? Proponents of this idea believe that abolishing parole would reduce the crime rate. Opponents think that parole works; inmates work harder at reform and good behavior if they know they will be rewarded with parole.

Your purpose is to write a multiple-paragraph essay, between 300 and 600 words, to be read by the National Board for Prison Reform. You take a position on whether the prison system should do away with parole. Be sure to defend your position with logical arguments and appropriate examples.

BSA 025
Intro to College Writing II

Persuasive Essay Topics

Choose one of the following as the topic for your persuasive essay:

1. Argue for or against giving your all to "getting ahead." Do the benefits of hard work (money, security, status, and so on) outweigh the disadvantages (pressure, loneliness, lack of free time, and so on)? Is "getting ahead" worth the time and effort it takes?

2. In today's world, many wives in two-parent families must work outside the home in order for the family to "make ends meet." Should husbands of wives who work outside the home help with the housework and child care?

3. It is a fact of life that drug addiction exists in our society. While the ultimate goal would be to wipe out such addiction, that will take time. In the meantime, many addicts share needles used to inject the drugs. This sharing of needles is one of the identifiable causes of the spread of AIDS. Should sterile needles be provided to addicts (at taxpayers' expense) to help halt the spread of AIDS?

4. Ivy Tech's mission is to give students specific skills that will enable them to compete successfully in today's job market. However, one of the skills required for being successful in most jobs is the ability to deal with people, whether coworkers or clients. Sociology is the study of how people interact. Should sociology be a required course at Ivy Tech?

5. Music changes from one generation to the next. My parents didn't enjoy the music I did when I was growing up. I don't enjoy all of the music my children listen to. Is popular music today more or less exciting than the music of ten (or twenty) years ago?

6. For many years, the legal system has based decisions on adoption rights on the assumption that only two-parent families are equipped to deal with the pressures of raising children. Today, many individuals are challenging that assumption. Should single people be allowed to adopt children?

7. There is a great deal of controversy today about proper penalties for those convicted of driving while intoxicated. What do you feel the punishment should be for those convicted of drunk driving?

7
Writing
Research
Papers

A mini research paper is a scholarly activity which involves all the processes of preparing a research study: topic identification, investigating source material, preparing research cards, developing a bibliography.... It is the first step of scholarship.

William G. Thomas, Los Angeles Trade Technical College, CA

From Sandra K. Hall, Corning Community College, NY

Research 11:
Information Superhighway

Name: _____   Grade: _____

Due: ___*Nov. 13*___

Planning a Research Essay (Essay 2)

> **Step 1:** Review your note cards and the highlights on articles.
>
> What interests you? _____
>
> What do you have enough information on that would develop into a good paper? (Examples of? Causes of? etc.)
>
> So, my *narrowed* FOCUS is: _____
>
> _____
>
> My PURPOSE is: _____
>
> **Step 2:** Determine a specific audience: _____
>
> **Step 3:** Go back to your notes and select the cards that have useful information.
>
> Arrange the cards in a logical order.
>
> Are you missing any important information? (If so, go find it!!)
>
> **Step 4:** Jot down some notes here that you want to remember for your conclusion.
>
> _____
>
> _____
>
> _____

Research 9:
Outline (Also on disk)

This is just a model. You will need to change this outline to fit the purposes you identified on previous page.

Title: _____

Paragraph 1:   Intro

- Make several statements that introduce us to the topic and get our attention.

- State your *thesis* as the last sentence.

Paragraph 2:   Body paragraph—your evidence

- Supporting detail 1

- Supporting detail 2

- Supporting detail 3

Paragraph 3:   Additional body paragraphs—As needed

- Supporting detail 1

- Supporting detail 2

- Supporting detail 3

Conclusion

- What do we do with the information we have just read?

- Why is it important? (Etc.)

You are now ready to get Research 11 approved and start writing your rough draft.

Remember that the rough and the final drafts will need a Works Cited page to be complete (this is Research 7).

Notecard

Author: *Ratan*
Page: *25*

Americans are spending almost as much on computer purchases as they are on televisions.

_____ Quote   ✔ Paraphrase   _____ Own idea

Paper

Most American families own television sets, but, what is surprising is the growing number of families who are buying computers. In fact, they are purchasing nearly an equal number of computers (Ratan 25). About 8 billion computers were sold in 1994. . . .

Works Cited

Ratan, Suneel. "A New Divide Between Haves and Have-nots?" *Time*, Spring 1995: 25–26.

FROM IDEA
to
LIBRARY SEARCH
to
ARTICLES on Topic
to
NOTES
to a
RESEARCH PAPER

Information Superhighway

Library Printout

Access No. 02295365
Title: A new divide between haves and have-nots?
Journal: Time (GTIM)
Vol. 145 no. 12 Date: Spring 1995 pp. 25–26
Subjects: Information superhighway; computers; social classes

Article

[TEXT]

MAKING SENSE OF LIBRARY PRINTOUTS:
How to Create a Works Cited List in MLA Style

Access: 01833183
Title: The little match girls
Authors: Anonymous
Journal: Economist
        Vol. 330   No. 7846   Date: Jan. 15, 1994   P. 38

Work Cited

"The Little Match Girls." Economist 15 Jan. 1994: 38.

Remember: If there is no author, start with the title.
Use " ."
Capitalize significant words.

Italicize titles of *magazines* and *books*.
Indent second and third lines if any part of the information
extends beyond one line.

If the magazine or paper is published weekly or daily, don't
forget to put the date before the month.

From Jane Wilson, Ivy Tech State College, IN

Research Paper
BSA 025

Selecting a Topic

The first step in writing a research paper is selecting a topic. The topic should be one that interests you, one that you wish to learn about. Most topics initially considered are too broad to fit the requirements of the paper and must be narrowed in scope. For example, the topic of "Sports" would be too general. You would need to narrow your subject to deal with a specific sport or with a specific happening in the world of sports. Once the topic is narrowed, ideas must be generated and organized. You might wish to refer to Chapters 2 and 3 in *Evergreen* for a review of how to generate and group ideas. The final step in this planning is the creation of a focused, directed thesis statement, and this must, of course, be a grammatically correct and clear sentence or group of sentences.

Topic (General): _____

Narrowed Topic: _____

Idea Generating and Organizing: Show this work on a separate, attached sheet.

Thesis Statement: _____

Research Paper
BSA 025
Intro to College Writing II

Summer 1995

1. The research paper will be 5 to 6 pages long (this includes the text of the paper but does *not* include the Works Cited page).

2. The paper must be double spaced.

3. The paper must have margins of approximately one (1) inch on all sides.

4. There will be no cover page, only an appropriate heading on the first page of the paper.

5. The material presented in the paper should be gathered from at least five sources.
   a. Only one encyclopedia may be used.
   b. Use recent material when possible.
   c. Materials may include books, magazines, reference books, pamphlets, videos, audiocassettes, interviews, newspapers, and so forth.

6. The Works Cited page and parenthetical reference should be according to the MLA format of documentation.

7. The paper will require the creation and submission of 50 notecards.

8. The final draft of the research paper must strive for accuracy of information, documentation, presentation, and grammar.

From William Thomas, Los Angeles Trade Technical College, CA

An Initiation into Research in English

Description

Re-search means to look again at a problem, topic, or subject of interest with new eyes, with a new mind putting information together. It requires that references be utilized and cited, or given credit as sources. It is the first step of scholarship—to seek truth or confirmation of hypotheses or facts to support a premise. It is not copying information indiscriminately and pretending the words are yours (this is a no-no).

A mini research paper is a scholarly activity that involves all the processes of preparing a research study: topic identification, investigating source material, preparing research cards, developing a bibliography, identifying appendices, and utilizing the Modern Language Association guidelines in organizing your study. All of the essential elements of a research study are present, except that instead of preparing 60 to 100 pages of research information, you need only prepare sample pages with examples of footnoting and citations on a footnote reference.

Topics

Topics may be of your own choosing. Suggested ideas include:

- An aspect or characteristic of a culture other than your own: religion, food, favorite sports, educational system, major products, and so forth

- A current event, such as the abortion issue, the presidential campaign, racism in television, the war on drugs, or equal educational opportunity

- A new invention or product for which you may want to predict a future, such as something relating to television, minihelicopters, wristwatch radios, lasers, sonar, pacemakers, or an item of your choice.

Length

Mini research papers should be five to eight pages, doublespaced, and typewritten or wordprocessed.

Footnotes

When you quote a source such as a book, magazine article, or interview, you should indicate that with a number beginning with 1 at the point of citation in your narration. In the appendices of your research paper, you should present the citation following the appropriate number on one or more pages titled "Footnotes." Listing such footnotes indicates that yours is a research paper, because you have sought out other materials relating to your topic of study.

Book, Article, or Interview Source Format

Book

Brown, Sam (Author), <u>Rio Bravo: The Great River</u> (Book), Bantam Books (Publisher), 1995 (Date), p. 123 (Specific source page).

Article in Book

Johnson, George (Author), "The Rolly Polly," (Article), <u>Being Plump</u> (Book in which article appears), Frankenstein & Sons (Publisher), 1823 (Date), p. 23 (Specific source page).

Article in Magazine or Newspaper

Albert, Frankie (Author), "Breaking the Fast Break" (Article), <u>Sportsnotes</u> (Magazine), July 7, 1989 (Date), Volume I, Number 7 (Specific publication), p. 87 (Specific source page).

Interviewee

Ho, Ron (Interviewee), Los Angeles Trade Technical College Student from Korea (Validation as expert on subject), February 4, 1991 (Date of interview).

or

Watkins, Johnathon, M.D. (Interviewee), Director of Abortion Clinic, USC Medical Center (Validation as expert on subject), January 23, 1990 (Date of interview).

Bibliograhy

The bibliography includes all sources investigated, whether or not quotes or footnotes are used. Even if you just thumbed through a book to see if it would be helpful, list it.

Organization of Paper

Title Page: Format

Title of Paper
Your Name
Date
Class

"In partial fulfillment of the requirements of the class of English 101, Dr. William G. Thomas"

Table of Contents: List subtopics and page numbers.

Topic	Page
Introduction	1
The Battle of Bulldogs	2
The Veterinarian Strikes	3
(and so on)	

Paper Organization:
 Introductory paragraph(s)
 Supportive paragraphs
 Concluding or summary paragraph(s)
 Appendices

Appendices: Appendices will include Footnotes, Bibliography, and any charts, maps, or graphs that support the topic.

Special Note: Researching should be fun. It is a literary adventure, much like Kojak or Columbo investigating a case, or Magic Johnson determining strategy against a basketball opponent.

Good luck.

Cultural Awareness Module—English 101

Using a Library for Research

A library—college, university, or public—is a researcher's best friend. The more specific a researcher is regarding a topic, the easier it is to locate useful material. The following library resources are recommended:

1. Encyclopedias—Encyclopedias provide broad, general information about a topic and list more specific references. Encyclopedias also suggest related topics to explore. There are various types of encyclopedias; some are subject oriented, while others are about geographical regions or specific fields of study.

2. The Card Catalogue—The card catalogue lists book subjects, titles, and authors held by the particular library.

3. Computer Searches—Many libraries provide the opportunity to search for information on a topic, author, or title from among one or more computer databases, as well as summarizing sources.

4. *Readers' Guide to Periodical Literature*—The *Readers' Guide* is a most useful resource that lists magazines, special newspaper features, and journal articles by subject.

5. Newspapers—Newspaper records can be used for information about events that occurred on or around certain dates. Newspapers are primarily viewed by researchers as secondary sources since information is quoted from or originated in another source.

6. Atlases and Maps—Atlases and maps are good places to start learning about the major cities, geography, and location of a country, as well as about its topography, environment, and potential strategic concerns.

7. The Reference Librarian—A library's reference librarian is usually a knowledgeable, specially trained professional who can identify resources, in addition to those suggested previously, that a particular library owns or has access to.

Sample Reference Card

Subject _____   Author _____

Article topic _____   Name of book or periodical _____

Publisher _____   Date of publication _____

Provide direct quotes, "_____," from resource or summary information and list page numbers.

8
Using Reading Selections

The reading selections are nicely varied, interesting, and at an appropriate level of difficulty as well. I am particularly pleased with the gender/ethnic/topic balance.

Meredith A. Wilson, Solano Community College, CA

The reading selections are excellent in both their interest level and the strategies they illustrate.

Muriel Brennan, College of San Marco, CA

From Keysha Ingram-Gamor, Montgomery College, MD

Using Narration, Description, Illustration, Process, and Comparison and Contrast in Developmental English

Rationale

In developmental classes, I find it particularly useful for the students to see that what they read is current and pertinent to the world around them. In addition, I structure the individual writing assignments to ultimately evolve into a full multiparagraph essay. Each paragraph represents a stage in the development of the final paper. In an effort to evidence relevancy and continuity, I seek out additional reading material that the authors in *Evergreen* are publishing or material about the authors themselves. Students respond well to this approach, with relevant, thoughtful, and personal dialogue and writing.

One essay to which students respond well is Brent Staples's "A Brother's Murder." Among other pedagogical objectives and in an effort to encourage outside reading, I found excerpts about other pieces he's written. I use "Between Two Worlds," an article that features Staples's latest book, from *Time* magazine (March 7, 1994), to establish currency and relevancy. Since students can often relate in one way or another to the feelings of loss as well as to the feelings of hopelessness, guilt, frustration, and utter desperation that Staples expresses in "A Brother's Murder," they respond well to "Between Two Worlds," which offers additional insight into the environment that destroys Blake and eats away at Brent himself. Students are particularly intrigued by this article for many reasons, not the least of which is the other author featured in "Between Two Worlds." For these students, it is especially interesting that these destructive phenomena are not isolated incidences; rather, they are bewildering facts that shed some light on the world from which some hide and others try to escape. Most effective is the fact that we always have those students who can take us further into this "netherworld" for further examination and others who can inquire and study in order to respond more effectively to the diverse experiences around them. In either case, we all come away with mixed feelings of the "high" we get from learning something new, and the desperation we feel when there's something that seems out of our immediate control.

To broaden the scope further, I focus on these themes of hopelessness, guilt, frustration, responsibility, and utter desperation as we tiptoe toward another alarming world, very similar to that of Blake and Brent. Students are often wondering what went wrong, in Blake's world, that didn't doom Brent to the same sentiments and consequential fate. Many students related to the portrait of Blake as out of control, in search of a final resting place, racing toward the unknown with blind speed. Enabled to see that Blake could have been anyone within that given set of circumstances or something similar, students are empowered to read and respond more critically in their discourse. "Between Two Worlds" provides students the opportunity to get a glimpse into the real issues that faced Brent and Blake, not only from Brent again but also from Nathan McCall.

At this juncture, I refer to some excerpts from McCall's *Makes Me Wanna Holler,* a book reviewed by Henry Louis Gates, Jr., and featured in *The New Yorker* under the title "Bad Influence." This series of reading material continues dialogue on many great themes, such as identity versus identification, finding a voice, family, relationships, determinism, victimization, realism, and so on. Since students generally respond so well to the text in *Evergreen* and are so involved in discussion, they really are able to grasp some more sophisticated literary terms and themes by examining these excerpts and articles. Interestingly enough, they remember this reading experience, and they are able to connect this experience with other readings as well as with their own experiences. All of a sudden, the students are reading for more than just an understanding of the plot. They begin to ask questions and share perceptions in ways they were incapable of before; furthermore, they are gaining confidence in their own interpretive abilities. Sharing new, in-depth insight is particularly exciting to students and me alike, for it truly takes their writing to a level they never thought they could get to.

Sample Writing Assignments (Separate due dates for each assignment)

1.
> Write about a time when you felt out of control. Describe only the event and your feelings. Do not expand any further at this point, for we are using this assignment as an opportunity to sharpen skills of narration and description. Pick your details carefully, choosing only the most accurate portrayal of what you experienced.
>
> *Length:* One paragraph of five to eight sentences.

2.
> Recall paper 1, about a time when you felt out of control. Explain either the steps you took to regain control or the stages of your succumbing to this overwhelming force in your life. What was your *response* to this feeling of losing control? What strategy did you develop in an effort to overcome the obstacle(s) you wrote about in paper 1?
>
> *Length:* One paragraph of five to eight sentences.

3.

> Write a paper in which you detail the response Blake (or Brent) had to his life-changing events. What did he do as he found himself in bad situations? Be sure to list as many examples as you can find in the text "A Brother's Murder."
>
> *Reminder:* Be sure to record the page number of each example you extract from the text.
>
> *Length:* One paragraph of five to eight sentences.

4.

> Reflect on the similarities and/or differences between how you and Blake or Brent, characters from "A Brother's Murder," respond to negative scenarios. Choose to discuss similarities or differences. (If you prefer, you may use the experiences of another author read in this course this semester.) Remember, this assignment calls for only one paragraph, so you will not have an opportunity to cover everything you might like.
>
> *Suggestion:* Write an informal outline in which you observe the characteristics of each person, and then choose which one you will use in your paper. I will collect the plans as well as the final paper.
>
> *Length:* One paragraph of five to eight sentences.

5.

> Write a multiparagraph essay in which you discuss the topic *Responding to Negative Experiences.*
>
> *Required Materials:* (There will be separate due dates for each stage of development.)
>
> - *Prewriting:* I will ask to see how you limited this topic to something specific, that is, your thesis statement.
> - *Organizing:* I will check for a formal outline for this paper.
> - *Revising and Editing:* I will look for an introduction, a conclusion, and a peer evaluation.
> - *Connecting:* I will expect you to include references to at least three relevant readings used in class so far, as well as your experiences developed in the previous paragraphs.
>
> *Length:* Three to five hundred words.

Readings

Current literature reinforces the idea of the positive effect reading and writing have on each other. I would strongly suggest that reading be incorporated in the course. The readings from the text should be assigned as part of class-discussion chapters or as part of the lecture component.

Sources include:

Congressional Digest—Monthly issues are devoted to one controversial congressional topic; pro and con arguments are presented by various U.S. representatives, senators, and special interest groups.

Editorials on File—A bimonthly newspaper editorial survey with a cumulative index.

Newsweek—Particularly the "My Turn" essays.

Social Issues Resources Series (SIRS)—Social and physical sciences; topical listing of articles from a large number of sources.

Time

USA Today—Particularly the editorial section, which often offers opposing viewpoints on a topic.

From Suzanne Doonan, Pennsylvania Institute of Technology, PA

English 100:
Selections to Read Aloud for Writing Prompts

"Learning to Write" by Russell Baker, in *Patterns Plus,* Houghton Mifflin, 1995
Students describe a time in their lives when they realized that they had a special skill or talent.

"The Magic Pebbles" from *A 2nd Helping of Chicken Soup for the Soul*
Students describe an experience or a person who seemed like a "pebble" but later became a "diamond" in their lives.

Selections from the following books:

Chicken Soup for the Soul by Mark Canfield and Victor Hansen, Health Communications, Deerfield, FL, 1995

Random Acts of Kindness and *More Random Acts of Kindness* by the editors of Conan Press, 1993
Students respond by relating personal experiences or the actions of others that have made a lasting impression on them.

The Book of Questions by Gregory Stock, Workman Publishing, 1987
Questions such as "Given the choice of anyone in the world, whom would you want as your dinner guest?
Some questions work well for dialogue journals. Students write a three to five sentence response and pass the paper to another student. Papers are passed among four or five students.

Politically Correct Bedtime Stories by James Finn Garner, MacMillan, 1994

From Sandra K. Hall, Corning Community College, CA

Using Readings with *Evergreen*

1. Find a sentence in the *factual article* attached from a reputable newspaper or weekly magazine (such as *Time*) that also includes a colorful description or uses an effective active verb.

2. Quote the sentence you have selected by writing it word-for-word in section 3 of this handout. Be sure to use quotation marks.

3. On the photocopy, highlight or <u>underline</u> the sentence you have quoted.

4. **Work Cited:** Include the bibliographic information in the order indicated (MLA style).

5. You must follow *all* directions to receive a grade.

Example from a *weekly* magazine:

---

2. Quote:

"As the bonfire crackles, the campers sit around in a circle and roast marshmallows and giggle."

4.   Work Cited

Gordon, Jeanne. "No Pampers, Pampering: A Cushy Camp for Moms." <u>Newsweek</u> 10 July 1989: 76.

Example from a *newspaper:* (no author provided)

---

2. Quote:

"Inside a cluster of plush buildings baked by the Silicon Valley sun, Apple Computer Inc. employees wearing sport shirts and jeans are readying products they hope will revive the company's breathtaking growth."

4.   Work Cited

"Apple's Future Clouded by Stepped-Up Competition." <u>Star Gazette</u> 17 July 1990: 1D.

Your Selection:

- Highlight your selected sentence.

- Copy the sentence you've selected, exactly as it appears in the article.

- BE SURE TO USE QUOTATION MARKS AT THE BEGINNING AND END of your quote.

---

2. My Quote:

_____

_____

_____

_____

_____

_____

_____

_____

---

4.   Work Cited

_____, _____. "_____

(Author's last name)   (First name)   (Put title of article in quotation

_____." _____

   marks & capitalize.)   (Title of magazine or paper, <u>underlined</u>)

_____, _____.

(Date Month Year)   (Complete pages of article)

Make sure you follow this pattern for citing the article:

EXAMPLE: Work Cited

Gordon, Jeanne. "No Pampers, Pampering: A Cushy Camp for Moms." <u>Newsweek</u> 10 July 1989: 76.

From Ann L. Lathrop, Lehman College, NY

Some Notes on Writing and Reading with *Evergreen*

Required Texts and Supplies

Evergreen with Readings by Susan Fawcett, 7th Edition

Bless Me, Ultima by Rudolfo Anaya (TQS Publications, Berkeley, CA)

An English dictionary with at least 50,000 entries: *American Heritage Dictionary* (highly recommended)

A looseleaf notebook with $8\frac{1}{2}$ x 11" paper (no spiral fringes, please) in which *all* the semester's work—notes, brainstorming, drafts, revisions, and Reader Responses—is kept.

Looseleaf section dividers

Index cards

Other Required Works

Genesis 1–3, King James Version

"Childhood and the Garden of Eden" by Marie Winn (Full publishing information follows.)

"Young Goodman Brown" by Nathaniel Hawthorne

Stand by Me, film available on videotape

I have used *Evergreen* successfully with lower and upper intermediate/lower advanced ESL classes in college developmental English programs. In the more advanced classes, the emphasis is on writing essays, especially persuasive ones, as students must show minimum competence in written English based on a 50-minute essay examination (the CUNY Writing Assessment Tests) with essay prompts that state a position and ask students to agree or disagree with that statement. I have found it helpful to expand some of the treatment of grammatical structures presented in *Evergreen,* because of the needs of ESL students. I then have the more advanced classes write paragraphs closely related to the book(s) that they are reading for the course, to practice rhetorical modes, and then extend the scope of their writing to full essays, using several of the modes as arguments to support a general thesis.

For example, when the class was reading Bless *Me, Ultima* by Rudolfo Anaya, a paragraph describing Ultima exercised present tense subject-verb agreement and followed the **descriptive** mode. Similarly, paragraphs

comparing and contrasting the golden carp and the black bass, and Narciso's garden and the Garden of Eden, correlated well with Chapter 10. Work later in the semester called on the students to compare and contrast the themes and features of *Bless Me, Ultima* and the film *Stand by Me*.

Stories about boys growing up may be separated by culture and other factors, but they may still have many themes and features in common. In what ways were *Bless Me, Ultima* and *Stand by Me* similar and in what ways were they different? Using specific examples from both the book and the film, compare and contrast these two works in a well-organized, well-edited essay.

In another instance, students used the modals *(would, could,* etc.), extending the work of Chapter 28 in a paragraph in the process mode to explain how they would train a *curandera /o* (herbalist), using Ultima's behavior toward Antonio as a guide. A later essay in the **persuasive** mode that worked well explored whether the student believed that such a person or such knowledge was applicable in current daily life.

"Ultima was a curandera, a woman who knew the herbs and remedies of the ancients, a miracle-worker who could heal the sick" (Anaya 4). At the same time, some people feared her and thought that she was a witch. Why might people have this opinion of such a person? Do you think that there is a place for this type of healer in our scientifically advanced society? Would you ever consult a person like her or advise someone else to do so? Why or why not?

Another such assignment that elicited good writing was one which called on knowledge of the book and drew on personal experience and observations and for which students were guided to use the modes of **cause and effect, process,** and **illustration** to discuss parental direction in career choice:

> Parents know their children's strengths and weaknesses better than anyone else, and they are familiar with the world into which their children are growing. Therefore, they should be the ones to decide their children's professions.
>
> Do you agree or disagree? Using the following essay elements, explain and illustrate your answer, drawing on your own experience, your observation of others, and your reading.
>
> 1. An **introductory** paragraph that states your position
>
> 2. A paragraph that supports your thesis by predicting the **consequence**
>
> 3. A paragraph that includes a **reference** to *Bless Me, Ultima* and an **illustration** from your own observation or experience to support your position
>
> 4. A well-developed **process** paragraph that supports your thesis and that tells how a career should be selected
>
> 5. A **concluding** paragraph that sums up your essay and gives the reader something interesting to think about

Along with the theme of friendship, the theme of coming of age or the loss of innocence is of interest to college students, and my more advanced students respond well to Genesis 1–3, read as background for Marie Winn's essay "Childhood and the Garden of Eden" (reprinted in *Purpose and Process* by Jeffrey D. Hoeper and James H. Pickering, New York: Macmillan, reprinted from *Children without Childhood*, Pantheon Books/Random House) and Nathaniel Hawthorne's "Young Goodman Brown." These pieces of writing are mind-stretching and linguistically challenging for most developmental and ESL English students and give a taste of the level of reading expected in college work. Thorough in-class discussion after students have read the pieces on their own can lead to a sense of mastery of and confidence in dealing with the material as well as pleasure in dealing with the ideas. Winn's essay also lends itself to a lesson in outlining and summary, necessary skills for college students.

Reading and Reader Response Schedule
for *Bless Me, Ultima*

Day	Date	Chapters *BMU*	Pages *BMU*	Reader Response	Grammar/Writing *Evergreen* Chapter
Tuesday	Feb. 1				Parts of Speech
Friday	Feb. 4	1,2	1–23 ⎫		1, 2
Tuesday	Feb. 8	3,4	25–43 ⎭ I		Sentence Functions
					24
Friday	Feb. 11	College Closed—Lincoln's Birthday			
Tuesday	Feb. 15	5–9	44–75	II	3, 5
Friday	Feb. 18	10	76–97 ⎫		25
Tuesday	Feb. 22	11	98–113 ⎭ III		6
Friday	Feb. 25	12, 13	114–136 ⎫		26, 7
Tuesday	Mar. 1	14	137–168 ⎭ IV		8
Friday	Mar. 4	15, 16	169–182 ⎫		27, 10
Tuesday	Mar. 8	17, 18	183–194 ⎭ V		13
Friday	Mar. 11	19, 20	207–225 ⎫		28
Tuesday	Mar. 15	21, 22	226–248 ⎭ VI		
Friday	Mar. 18	Midsemester Exam			29
Tuesday	Mar. 22				30
Friday	Mar. 25	Library Session			
		SPRING VACATION			
Tuesday	Apr. 5				32
Friday	Apr. 8				
Tuesday	Apr. 12				33
Friday	Apr. 15				
Tuesday	Apr. 19				34
Friday	Apr. 22				
Tuesday	Apr. 26				35
Friday	Apr. 29				36
Tuesday	May 3				
Friday	May 6	Department Final—Essay			
Tuesday	May 10	WAT (Program Exit Exam)			
		CELT (Grammar Proficiency Exam)			

9
Sample Syllabi

The separation of the grammar and writing sections is very good and is one of the advantages of using *Evergreen*. With the organization the way it is, the instructor is free to assign grammar and sentence structure along with the readings and the writing practices.

Debra Anderson, Indian River Community College, FL

Evergreen's units logically classify all the appropriate areas of concentration. Though I seldom assign the units in sequential order, I find that it's easy to mix and match chapters without sacrificing continuity.

Debra Callen, Harold Washington College, IL

English 0250—Compensatory College Skills
Fall 2002

Instructor: Kathleen Beauchene, Assistant Professor   Office Hours: M 10–11 a.m.
Lincoln English Department, Room 1214   T 11:15 a. m.–1 p.m.
Voice mail: 333-7389; English Dept. 333-7372   Th 11:15a.m. -1 p.m.
email: kbeauchene@ccri.edu

Goals

At the end of this course, you should be able to:

- Determine your purpose for writing

- Choose and limit a subject

- Generate ideas for your subject

- Write a topic sentence

- Write a paragraph using examples, facts, details and so on to support a topic sentence

- Organize and connect ideas

- Write a focused paragraph that expresses your point of view in sentences that are complete and grammatically correct

- Evaluate and rewrite a paragraph using the techniques of support, unity, coherence, and sentence skills

- Demonstrate readiness for Fundamentals of Writing (English 1050)

Course Policies
Materials:

- Book: *Evergreen: A Guide to Writing,* 7th Edition
- Three-ring binder
- Composition paper
- Folder
- Dividers
- Dictionary

Requirements: During the course, you will be required to:

- Keep a Writer's Notebook

- Submit three revised paragraphs from your Writer's Notebook for mid-term evaluation

- Write eight to ten paragraph-length assignments

- Take two major unit tests

- Complete homework assignments

- Take a quiz after each chapter has been completed and discussed in class

- Contribute to class by sharing writing and evaluating writing

- Work with the Writing Center if the instructor requires

Attendance:

Obviously, students will be absent for various reasons. Whatever the reason, you are still responsible for the homework. Please email me for missed work. Students with frequent absences are unable to meet the course requirements outlined above. Consequently, they are likely to receive an unsatisfactory grade. After your third absence, I will meet with you to discuss your course status. After 6 absences, I will ask you to drop the course.

Grading:

1. *Tests* Tests will be graded in the traditional manner (for example, 85%). A grade of 70% is considered passing. If you receive less than 70% on a quiz, you will be allowed to take an alternative quiz provided that you prove to me that you have reviewed the material. "Proof" may include a conference with me, a completed worksheet, a completed handout from an approved Internet site, a Writing Center conference, and so on.

2. *Writing assignments, which will all be computer generated* Writing assignments will receive a variety of checks (✔+, ✔, and ✔–).

   A check (✔) is considered passing; therefore, if a writing assignment receives an "R" (rewrite), you will need to rewrite the assignment after meeting with me to discuss it. If the writing assignment does not improve significantly after you rewrite it, you will receive a ✔–.

3. *Final grade:* "S" (Satisfactory) or "U" (Unsatisfactory).
   You will receive an "S" provided you:

   - Receive at least a ✔ on the final in-class writing

   - Receive at least a ✔ on 75% of paragraph writing assignments

   - Pass 75% of the tests and quizzes with at least a grade of 70%

   - Attend class on a regular basis

Tentative Syllabus

The following syllabus will be adjusted to fit the needs of the students.

Week	Writing Concept	Sentence Skills	
1	Course and Student Introduction	Appendix	Spelling (on-going work)
2	Getting Started Techniques Brainstorming/Listing/Freewriting	Ch. 24	The Sentence
3	Introduction to the Topic Sentence	Ch. 26	Avoiding Errors
4	Practicing Writing the Topic Sentence	Ch. 26	Avoiding Errors
5	Supporting the Topic Sentence	Ch. 25	Coordination
6	Revising Techniques	Ch. 25	Subordination
7	Conference Week — Writer's Notebook due		
8 & 9	Coherence-organizing Information	Ch. 31	Pronouns
10	Using Examples	Ch. 27	Present Tense/Agreement
11	Using Description	Ch. 35	Comma
12	Using Process	Ch. 34	Apostrophe
13	Using Comparison/Contrast	Ch. 36	Mechanics
14	Using Persuasion		Open
15	Course Summary		As Needed

COURSE OUTLINE

Course Title:	Introduction to College Writing II
Course Number:	ENG 025 (32 sessions)
Prerequisites:	Successful completion of ENG 024 or demonstrated competency through appropriate assessment (ASSET 38–40, COMPASS 52–69)
Program:	Basic Skills
Division:	General Education and Support Services
Credit Hours:	3
Contact Hours:	3

Catalogue Course Description

Builds on the competencies learned in ENG 024 and prepares the student for entry into ENG 111. Enables beginning college writers to expand control of the writing process through writings that are focused, organized, and well developed. Requires students to demonstrate increased proficiency in the use of standard writing conventions.

General Course Objectives:

Upon successful completion of this course, the student will be expected to:

1. Demonstrate increased control of the writing process evidenced by multiparagraph writings that are focused, organized, and well developed.

2. Demonstrate increased self-confidence as a writer through interaction with peers and participation in collaborative groups.

3. Demonstrate use of the paragraph in the context of the essay.

4. Write well-developed essays with attention to voice, audience, and purpose.

5. Demonstrate increased proficiency in the application of grammar and mechanics in the writing process.

6. Demonstrate the research process by writing a paper that includes selection evaluation and use of appropriate documentation of sources.

Methods of Evaluation:

GESS Division Grading Guidelines:
    A = 90–100
    B = 80–89
    C = 70–79
    F = 69 and below

• Note: College policy requires successful completion (C or better) of this course before proceeding to the next developmental course or to any general education or programmatic course for which it is a prerequisite. Students who do not successfully complete this course will be required to repeat the course in the next semester.

The course grade for ENG 025 will be based on the following criteria:

Paragraphs of introduction	100 points
Informative essay	100
Persuasive essay	100
Selected exercises	100
Research paper working outline	100
Works Cited page	100
Research note cards (50)	100
Research paper	200
Final memo	100
	1000 points

• Regular attendance is necessary for successful completion of all college courses. Your instructor will provide you with a copy of his or her policy regarding attendance and make-up work

Suggested Texts:

Fawcett, Susan. *Evergreen with Readings.* 7th Edition. Houghton Mifflin Company.
Charnigo, Richard. *From Sources to Citation.* Harper Collins.

• If you need course adaptations or accommodations because of a disability, if you have emergency medical information to share with me, or if you need special arrangements in case the building must be evacuated, please make an appointment with me as soon as possible.

• The instructor retains the prerogative of changing or adjusting the course syllabus to best accommodate the pace of progression and the needs of the students.

ENG 025—32 sessions

Class Calendar

Students are expected to read assigned chapters before the material is covered in the classroom and to pay close attention to due dates for papers.
SC = *From Sources to Citation*

Session	Class Activity
1	Orientation to class
	Safety Rules
	Syllabus Review
	Attendance policies
	Textbook preview
	Getting acquainted exercise
2	Chapter 1 – Exploring the Writing Process (p. 3)
	Chapter 2 – Prewriting to Generate Ideas (p. 8)
3	Chapter 3 – Process of Writing Paragraphs (p. 21)
	Chapter 4 – Achieving Coherence (p. 44)
4	Essay of Introduction assigned
	Word Processing Exercise
5	**Paragraphs of Introduction due**
	Chapter 5 – Paragraph of Illustration (p. 67)
	Chapter 6 – Paragraph of Narration (p. 76)
6	Chapter 7 – Paragraph of Description (p. 84)
	Chapter 8 – Paragraph of Process (p. 92)
7	Chapter 9 – Paragraph of Definition (p. 102)
	Chapter 10 – Paragraph of Comparison and Contrast (p. 115)
8	Chapter 11 – Paragraph of Classification (p. 132)
	Chapter 12 – Paragraph of Cause and Effect (p. 141)
9	Chapter 14 – The Process of Writing an Essay (p. 169)
	Chapter 15 – Types of Essays (p. 198)
10	Chapter 16 – The Introduction, the Conclusion, and the Title (p. 222)
	Informative Essay assigned
11	Chapter 20 – Revising for Consistency and Parallelism (p. 267)
	Chapter 21 – Revising for Sentence Variety (p. 283)
12	**Informative Essay due**
	Chapter 22 – Revising for Language Awareness (p. 312)
	Chapter 23 – Putting Your Revision Skills to Work (p. 328)
13	Chapter 19 – Writing Under Pressure: The Essay Examination (p. 253)

14   Chapter 13 – Persuasion (p. 150)
          Persuasive Essay assigned

15   Chapter 17 – Special College Skills: Summary and Quotation
                    (p. 230)

16   **Persuasive Essay due**
          Review Day: Grammar and Spelling

17   Introduction to the research paper and process
          SC 1 – What is Research? (p. 1)

18   SC 2 – What is a Good Topic? (p. 7)
          Research paper assigned

19   SC 3 – What the Library Has to Offer (p. 19)

20   Introduction to electronic sources

21   SC 4 – The Outline as an Organizing Device (p. 31)

22   Discuss choice of sources and organization for research paper
          Working outline assigned

23   **Working Outline due**
          SC 6 – Documenting Your Sources (p. 47)

24   Group work on Works Cited entries: Bring sources to class!

25   No class session – instructor will be available for individual
          consultations on Works Cited page.

26   **Works Cited page due**
          SC 5 – Taking Notes: Using Other People's Ideas and
                    Information (p. 37)

27   Discussion on note taking
28   SC 7 – Putting it All Together: Rough Draft to Final Product
                    (p. 77)

29   **Note Cards due**
          Final discussion and questions on the research paper

30   No class session – instructor will be available for individual
          consultations on the research paper

31   **Research paper due**
          Discussion of Final Memo

32   **Final Memo due**

From Cliff Gardiner, Augusta College, GA

Course Description.
DEVELOPMENTAL WRITING II
Text: *Evergreen with Readings*

Typical Week-by-Week Progression Through the Text

Week 1:	Chapters 2 and 3
Week 2:	Chapter 14
Week 3:	Chapter 15; Chapter 16
Week 4:	Chapter 24; Chapter 25
Week 5:	Chapter 25; Chapter 26
Week 6:	Chapter 11 and Chapter 15; Chapter 20
Week 7:	Chapter 35
Weeks 8 and 9:	We do practice tests of grammar, mechanics, and usage in preparation for our state-mandated Collegiate Placement Examination (CPE), which students are required to pass in order to exit the course and go on to Freshman English.
Week 10:	Students write two 45-minute exam essays on topics sentenced by the instructor from a list distributed to students a week earlier; those who pass at least one essay proceed to phase two of the final exam, the CPE.

The "Laboratory" Component of the Course

Students are required to work independently on any aspect of writing they choose, for a total of two hours per week. I offer them several contexts for this individualized work; working in chapters from *Evergreen* that we won't be covering as an entire class (many choose this option), tutorial help in Augusta College's Writing Lab, or working in any of several supplementary texts and workbooks that we house in our library and our Learning Center.

Writing Assignments

Students write at least one essay per week. The first is done out of class, most of the others in class; students select one or two essays to revise out of class. They are encouraged to submit one of these essays to be considered for publication in *BrainPower,* a biannual magazine of developmental students' writing and artwork.

Students write primarily on assigned topics, although I always allow them a choice. We begin with (to use James Kinneavy's terms) expressive topics and progress to more referential topics.

English 100: Basic Writing

COURSE SYLLABUS

Content overview (subject to modification as warranted)

Week	Class Content	Homework Assignments
1	Diagnostic essay 1; introductory course overview	Appendix 2 Diagnostic essay 2
2	Outlining principles; intro to eight parts of speech and the sentence	Chapters 24, 30, 32, 33
3	Discovering the paragraph: brainstorming, selecting & narrowing topic sentence, ideas, writing, revising; coherence	Chapters 2, 3, 4 **Paper 1** (Chapter 7, Description)
4	Process of subordination & coordination	Chapters 21–22
5	Sentence errors: run-ons, splices, fragments; review of mechanics	Chapters 23, 30 **Paper 2** (Chapter 7, Narrative)
6	**Review:** outlining, writing the paragraph, development, sentence sense **Mid-Term Examination**	
7	Editing process: proofreading methods, double-correction method, writing folder setup, revisions	Chapters 20, 21, 22 Consistency, variety, language awareness
8	The process paragraph	Chapter 8
9, 10	Verbs (agreement): subject-verb agreement, troublesome verbs, separating verbs and subjects, agreement in questions and clauses	Chapters 27, 31 **Paper 3** (Process)
11	Verb tenses (usage): present and past tense; the past participle **Workshops: Revisions, rewrites, CES work**	Chapters 27, 28, 29
12	Improving the paragraph: overall cumulative review	Chapters 34, 35, 36
13	The essay: mechanics (MLA), thesis, intro, title, conclusion; the tour-paragraph essay	Chapters 14, 15F, 16
14	The essay question: how to read, answer, and write a four- to five-paragraph essay answer (preparation for exit)	Ch. 19 **Paper 4** (Comparison-Contrast essay)

15   General review: practice workshop for exit
       essay, objective final, and rewrites

Final examination/collection of writing folders

From Nancy Zebko, Wayne County Community College, MI

English 109, Basic Writing Skills II

Step 1

I administer the Diagnostic Test accompanying the text that covers grammar, usage, and mechanics skills. Based on student results, I recommend intensive Learning Lab work, including individual tutoring, group sessions, and independent work materials (computer programs, video and audio materials).

I administer a mid-term skills assessment and a final mastery test. A passing grade is 70% or better.

Step 2

I introduce the students to Microsoft Word on our Macintosh computers and assign the paragraphs on pages 39–40. For this assignment and all that follow, I ask students to submit their choice of a prewriting exercise, rough draft, and final copy.

Step 3

Class time consists of discussion of readings (one each week), chapters that fit our needs (this varies, depending on the types of errors I am spotting in papers), discussion of rhetoric (the first half of our 15-week course concentrates on paragraph writing, the second half on short essays). My students generate many papers, creating a writing portfolio for themselves. I collect their folders for official grading three times during the semester, reading all papers and grading the ones they have chosen as "best."

Step 4

A student's final grade is a synthesis of all the areas covered in class, plus level of participation and attendance. Lots of independent textbook reading is required in my class. I encourage students to check any pages we haven't covered in class against my text or with the tutor. I have a very close relationship with the Learning Lab and believe that students need to view their work from as many perspectives as possible. Probably half the time spent on our class is spent at the lab.

Weekly Schedule

Evergreen = E   *Interactions* = I

Exercises in E will be assigned on a weekly basis, some as in-class work and others as homework.

Week 1	Introductions, Business I, p. 528 "The Man in the Water" Reading Handouts E, Ch. 14 The Process of Writing an Essay
Week 2	E, Chs. 5 and 15A Illustration E, Ch. 2 Generating Ideas E, Ch. 16A The Introduction
Week 3	E, Chs. 13 and 15H Persuasion I, p. 471 "Electronic Gizmos Make Us Stupid" I, p. 475 "The Beep Goes On" E, Ch. 16 B and C The Conclusion and The Title E, Ch. 25 Coordination and Subordination **ESSAY 1 DUE: Illustration**
Week 4	Persuasion, cont. I, p. 458 "Television Addiction"/Reading Handout I, p. 461 "Why I Quit Watching Television" I, p. 450 "Taking a Byte Out of Privacy" "Coordination and subordination" extra practice **ESSAY 2 DUE: Persuasion**
Week 5	Research Paper Library Tools Using research material Endnotes and Bibliography
Week 6	E, Chs. 6 and 15B Narration E, Ch. 35 B, C, D The Comma E, p. 518 "A Brother's Murder"
Week 7	In-class workshop on research paper E, Ch. 29 The Past Participle **ESSAY 3 DUE: Narration**
Week 8	Review for Midterm Exam Midterm Exam (2 parts: Essay and Mechanics)
Week 9	E, Chs. 10 and 15F Comparison/Contrast I, p. 264 "Love Is Never Enough" E, Ch. 24 The Simple Sentence (identifying subjects and verbs) E, Ch. 27 Present Tense/Agreement **ESSAY 4 DUE: Comparison/Contrast (in-class essay)**

Print and Electronic Resources
for Instructors of Developing Writers

Print

Periodicals

College Composition and Communication. Urbana, IL: NCTE/CCCC. Quarterly, beginning 1950. Subscriptions: 1111 Kenyon Road, Urbana, IL 61801.

College English. Urbana, IL: NOTE College Section. Eight times a year, beginning 1939. Subscriptions: 1111 Kenyon Road, Urbana, IL 61801.

Journal of Basic Writing. New York: City University of New York Instructional Resource Center. Twice a year, beginning 1978. Subscriptions and submissions: Instructional Resource Center, City University of New York, 535 East 80th Street, New York, NY 10021.

Research in the Teaching of English. Athens: University of Georgia, NCTE Committee on Research. Three times a year, beginning 1967. Subscriptions: 1111 Kenyon Road, Urbana, IL 61801.

Teaching English in the Two-Year College. Urbana, IL: NCTE. Quarterly, beginning 1974. Subscriptions: 1111 Kenyon Road, Urbana, IL 61801.

The Writing Instructor. Los Angeles: University of Southern California. Quarterly, beginning 1981. Subscriptions and submissions: 817 W. 34th Street, Fourth Floor, University of Southern California, Los Angeles, CA 90089.

General Bibliographies

Enos, Theresa, ed. *Sourcebook for Basic Writing Teachers.* New York: Random House, 1987.

Lindemann, Erika. *Longman Bibliography of Composition and Rhetoric: 1984–1985 and 1986.* New York: Longman, 1987, 1988.

Tate, Gary, ed. *Teaching Composition: Twelve Bibliographic Essays.* Fort Worth: Texas Christian University Press, 1987.

Electronic Resources

http://teams.lacoe.edu (Teams Distance Learning)

http://www.ed.gov/pubs/ResearachrsGuide/Services.html (U.S. Dept of Education)

http://www.mala.bc.ca/www/wac/wac.htm (Writing Across the Curriculum)

http://www.ncte.org/tetyc/te0243toc.shtml (Teaching English in the Two Year College)

http://college.hmco.com/devenglish/dolphinville (Houghton Mifflin's own Developmental Writing web site) http://planet.tvi.cc.nm.us/ctac/teachideas/wk1ju199.htm (Teaching Ideas)

http://w3.tvi.cc.nm.us/~nseeking/cwc99.htm (Shared teaching resources)

http://www.mla.org (Modern Language Association official site)

http://www.nade.net (Home site of the National Association for Developmental Education

http://www.slcc.edu/wc/teacher/teach.htm (Teaching resources)

http://www.lib.berkeley.edu/TeachingLib/Guides/Internet/FindInfo.html (Internet research strategies)

http://www.albany.edu/cetl/resources/pedagogy/plagiarism.html (Teacher's guide to plagiarism)

http://college.hmco.com/devenglish/resources/links/instructors/index.html (Houghton Mifflin Instructor Resource Center)

Submissions Wanted
from
Students and Instructors

From Students:

As students are essential members of the Evergreen Community, we invite them to send us their comments on any aspect of writing, writing classes, or English classes in general—what they like or dislike, what works best, what just doesn't ever seem to work, what their life goals are, and how they think writing and English will help them achieve those goals. In sum, we are open to receiving just about anything students want to say that is related to *Evergreen,* writing, or the study of English. We will publish a portion of the student submissions in the next edition of *The Evergreen Community.*

From Instructors:

Please send us your teaching ideas, reading lists, course outlines, or syllabi for possible inclusion in the Eighth Edition of *The Evergreen Community.* We want to keep the community growing, and making this collection as interesting and useful as possible is an important part of making that happen.

Options for Getting Your Submissions to Us

FAX: Please include a copy of your completed submission form with your submission and fax them to us at 617.351.1134.

Internet: We welcome email submissions. To send us your submission using this option, please provide—in your own format—all of the relevant information that we ask for on the submission form and send your submission to the following address: Peter_Mooney@hmco.com.

Thank you!!!!

The Evergreen Community
Submission Form

Please complete and enclose this form with your *Evergreen Community* submission.

Instructors and Students

Name _____

School _____

Address _____

_____

Phone _____ Fax _____

Internet _____

Instructors Only

Course(s) in which you have used *Evergreen* or *Evergreen with Readings* (please specify which version)

_____

_____

_____